FIELDS OF
DREAMS
AND
BROKEN
FENCES

AARON MOORE

FIELDS OF
DREAMS
AND
BROKEN
FENCES

DELVING INTO THE MYSTERY WORLD
OF NON-LEAGUE FOOTBALL

First published by Pitch Publishing, 2022

Pitch Publishing
A2 Yeoman Gate
Yeoman Way
Worthing
Sussex
BN13 3QZ
www.pitchpublishing.co.uk
info@pitchpublishing.co.uk

A CIP catalogue record is available for this book
from the British Library.

ISBN 978-1 80150 100 2

Typesetting and origination by Pitch Publishing
Printed and bound in Great Britain by TJ Books, Padstow

Contents

Acknowledgements

THIS BOOK was a sheer joy to work on.

I owe thanks to many people who gave up their time to talk to me and share their stories: Mike McGraa (Vauxhall Motors), Adam Jackson-Nocher (Waltham Rabble), Andrzej Perkins (Walthamstow), Steve Castle (Royston Town), Jobi McAnuff (Leyton Orient), Joe Perrett (Harlow Town Ladies), Joe Sheehan (Ipswich Town Women), Jason Alex Hill (District Line Railway), Neil Smythe (Hashtag United), Daniel Potter (Chichester City), Adam Connelly (Harlow Town Reserves), Phil Annets (FA Cup Factfile), Cem Toygar (Piccadilly FC), Darren Fielding (South Western Railway), Becky Shephard (Stevenage Women), Marc White (Dorking Wanderers), Nick Robinson and Les Bradd (plus others at Notts County), Daniel Merrix (Upton Park Ladies), James Bransgrove (Enfield FC), Charlie Mann (Hadley FC), Paul Halsey (Ware FC), Gary Cohen (Dunmow Town), Joe Cassidy, Gary Price and Sophia Axelsson (plus others at Clapton CFC).

A huge thanks to Bill Badger for agreeing to write the foreword and sharing his own story of why he loves non-league, for giving the book a once-over and for sharing his ideas (without which the book would not be the same!).

Thanks to Jane Camillin at Pitch Publishing for helping make this book a reality.

Thanks to Ollie Bayliss of the *Non-League Show* for providing an insight into covering the FA's decisions and sharing his thoughts.

Thanks to Ross Halls, Max Reeves, Garry Strutt, and Andrzej Perkins for the use of their images.

Foreword by Bill Badger, Walthamstow FC's Inclusion and Equality Officer

I WAS attracted back to non-league football out of a sense of community. I grew up in Walthamstow and, even though we'd moved away, I still felt an attachment to E17. In 2018, Waltham Forest FC changed their name to Walthamstow FC, and the name change pulled me in. It was a chance to maintain a link with where I had grown up. It was also a break from tribal, win at any cost, professional football.

I hadn't intended to start following non-league football. If anything, I was apprehensive when I found out just how far down the non-league pyramid they were. I imagined they were a division or two below what we used to call the Conference. A couple of good seasons and you could be at the top of the non-league game. What was worth playing for when you are four leagues below the Conference? So, I didn't bother with any league games and went to an FA Cup tie instead, a serious competition with glamour and potential glory.

There was to be no glory. Stow were knocked out of the competition by Beaconsfield from two leagues above them. They still had a decent enough afternoon. I enjoyed being able to chat to the linesman during the game and hearing every word said by the players and the referee. My enjoyment wasn't consumed by the result or embroiled in petty rivalries. It wasn't enough to make me want to follow the team every week, but it could provide a welcome breath of fresh air away from the heavy industry of professional football if I went every now and again.

The air became intoxicating. I quickly realised you don't follow non-league football, you join it and become a part of it. The faces around you quickly become familiar, as does your own to the people around you and the players themselves. Fans are important to professional clubs on a collective basis. Clubs have to bring in the volume of fans they need through the turnstiles to keep their business afloat. Everyone involved in non-league is valued because of the contribution they make as individuals to the clubs, the players and each other.

Non-league teams are dependent on players who commit to maintaining their abilities and fitness levels that enable them to perform to a good standard. They fit their training and matches around their education and daily working lives. That commitment is matched off of the pitch by armies of volunteers who keep the clubs running. Any time and any skill that a fan can offer to a club is gratefully received by officials. I should know – when I was ten years old I first went to watch Leyton Wingate and on the following Bank

Holiday Monday I was back at the ground responding to their plea for fans to come and help them paint the fences. Club officials spend hours completing administration and undertaking a multitude of tasks to ensure that teams have somewhere to play and train, have kit to play in and have fans there to watch them.

Coaches also give up their time to support players in their football careers and in their lives, taking responsibility for the development and wellbeing of the young men and women they send out to play football. And whether they number two dozen or 200, the teams are supported by groups of hardcore fans who unfailingly back their clubs financially and emotionally. They will be there in all weathers, in joy and in sorrow, willing their teams on to success, whatever success looks like for them. For some that will be promotion, for others it's avoiding relegation, and for some it will simply be getting a team out on the pitch for another season.

Whatever league your team is in you are all part of a fantastic experience, whether you are giving your support, selling raffle tickets, running the gate, putting posters up in local pubs, painting fences, stewarding, playing, coaching, or paying the bills. No one is in it for the money or glory because there is little of either to go around. All of us are there because, through all of the highs and lows, we just love the game.

1

Null and Void

THE DECISION by the Football Association to null and void the 2019/20 season hurt many clubs. The coronavirus outbreak was declared a global pandemic weeks before football was suspended, but once it was, the FA took the rash decision in voiding the season while also wiping any trace from their records. This meant that the campaign was ended with immediate effect, but there was no conclusion to it, putting promotion, relegation, and the domestic cups up in the air. While many teams were close to achieving promotion, two had mathematically secured it – Vauxhall Motors and Jersey Bulls. These clubs were hit the hardest.

It made the FA look more out of touch with the lower leagues than they already were. Originally, a decision had been made for the Premier League, English Football League and National League, but the lower tiers were left to their own accord. A decision on how the 'elite' leagues should end wasn't reached straight away, with the prospect of promotion, relegation and play-offs being done on points-per-game, but non-league was kicked to the kerb without regard. The hard-working part-timers were not classed on the same level as the 'elite' players, and it made the decision even tougher to take. The leagues were sensible. Many, when left to make their own decisions, postponed fixtures until further notice, while the National League continued to play their games. The Football Association's decision to allow individual leagues to decide their own fate was an incredibly risky move, although many complied with the Government's advice. There was no immediate decision to ban sporting events, so for the safety of all involved, leagues implemented guidelines and began to postpone leagues.

Vauxhall had played out one of the small amount of games on 14 March, just before all fixtures were postponed, and it was an important win. The celebrations echoed around as the club celebrated one of the first promotions of the season. The vital three points against West Didsbury & Chorlton meant that, even if they lost their remaining seven games, they would still finish fourth and in a promotion spot, but they didn't have that on their mind.

'It was a difficult decision to take. I think it was a rash decision and one that needed more time. I am actually angry. The boys did incredibly well this season, but it has been taken from them. A decision out of our hands,' said Vauxhall manager Mike McGraa.

Not much was known about the virus in the early stages, so it was difficult to know what the best solution was going forward. Mike knew that a decision had to be made, but he questioned why decisions were made quicker on the lower leagues compared to the National League and above. What was the harm in waiting?

'I think they could have delayed everything. The decision to expunge the results means the season was never in existence. I think they could have waited another two or three weeks and gone down any number of different routes rather than null and voiding the season.'

There was a lot of talk about decisions being made on an average of points gained per game across the fixtures already played. When matches were postponed in March, many clubs had played the majority of theirs and only had nine to play out of a 36- or 38-game season. That meant that a decision on points-per-game would give a fair indication of a team's season.

'Points-per-game was the fairest way to do it. I know it would have upset those who missed out on going up and caused some to go down, but if you look at the season as a whole; if you're in the bottom three, you are there for a reason. It's the same if you are in the top four,' said McGraa.

Although many clubs had games in hand due to the harsh winter weather and cup runs, not many leagues would change. Ascot United sat top of the Combined Counties Football League Premier Division, and although Spelthorne Sports had a game in hand, they couldn't have overtaken the leaders. Instead, Spelthorne were just a single point ahead of Knaphill, who had three games in hand over them. The North West Counties League Premier Division was a different story. 1874 Northwich, Warrington Rylands and Bootle sat in the three promotion places, with Charnock

Richard trailing behind. Although Charnock were level on points with third-placed Bootle, the team above them had four games in hand while Rylands had one and Northwich had two. The points-per-game system would have promoted all three, and rightly so.

McGraa said, 'I understand people have games in hand, but they are there for a reason. The games you've played represent where you are. The leagues don't lie. You don't have to have play-offs, just promote the top two. Do promotions and relegations because it's about reward and failure. The teams that haven't had a good season or have struggled have got a reprieve while those who have succeeded are getting nothing.'

Jersey Bulls were in the exact same boat as Vauxhall, and it was difficult not to feel for them. Both clubs had shared their stories on similar platforms; the radio and the *Non-League Paper* heard them. McGraa had contacted the Bulls' manager to share his sympathy.

He said, 'I spoke to the manager. We don't know each other, but we spoke to the same people on the radio and in the paper, so numbers were passed around and I reached out. He's a really nice fella and I'm as gutted for them as I am for us. They spent a lot of money, obviously, getting people over to Jersey cost them a lot.'

A condition of the Bulls' acceptance into the National League System meant they would have to cover the costs of visiting teams and officials. They had to do this as they are based on the island of Jersey in the English Channel, so teams had to get flights and ferries across on a matchday.

They had also spent a lot of money to get themselves over to mainland England for away games, a cost that limited teams faced.

'I'm gutted for everyone affected. Especially the clubs that were nearly there [to getting promoted] and knew it was going to happen. They've been let down by the decision as well. Points-per-game was the way to go,' said McGraa.

The Vauxhall manager had tried to make sense of the decision as he contemplated what was next for his team. It had only been Steps 3-6 of the National League System (levels 7-10 of the English football pyramid) that were voided almost immediately, but for these teams, it was more than football. Although players earned at that level, it was merely pocket money and not enough to live on, so they were part-time footballers with time and expenses sacrificed throughout the season. For Vauxhall, the decision affected them as they sat at Step 6. McGraa reflected on the season but remained disappointed at the outcome.

'This season consisted of loads of work. This wasn't just over a season, but two seasons in the making. We've had the same group of lads over that period of time and just added quality to the squad. All the lads had their jobs and knew what they needed to do. They worked and trained hard week in, week out and we've been the best team in the league by a mile. It's disappointing it has ended like this,' he continued. 'We were never a Step 6 team. The players we have at the club make up a Step 4 or 5 team, and we are good enough for that level. I know all my players aspire to play higher and that's what we achieved this season, but now, that's been taken away. I expect it to be a struggle to keep hold of many of these players and I'm expecting clubs to come in for them. It's going to be hard to bounce back from this.'

Although it was frustrating, McGraa had moments he had enjoyed to reflect on. On top of flying in the league, Vauxhall had also enjoyed a good run in the FA Vase.

'I really enjoyed the last game we played [a 1-0 victory over West Didsbury & Chorlton]. It summed up our season in a single game. We were tough to beat and worked hard. We played some good football, but also grinded out results, so that was the most satisfying. I also enjoyed the FA Vase [third round] game against Newcastle Benfield when we were a depleted team [with suspensions and injuries]. We managed to beat a really good side 2-0 when we had five or six first-team players missing. That got us to the last 32.'

Their run in the FA Vase was brought to an end in the fourth round by eventual winners Hebburn Town with a narrow 1-0 loss, but the cups weren't their main priority. The Vase had been a competition of mixed results for the Motormen. The club's best run saw them reach the semi-finals in the 1999/2000 season, but in recent times, they hadn't reached those heights. Their run from the 2014/15 to 2017/18 saw them fail to get past the second qualifying round until a good run in 2018/19 saw them battle their way through to the second round proper. Vauxhall had started that run with progression past Longridge Town before facing Cheadle Town in the following round. The game had ended 2-2, leading the Motormen on to a 6-0 replay victory at home to set up a tie with Seaham Red Star. With a 4-0 victory over the County Durham side, the club's run came to an end at the hands of Runcorn Town. The 2019/20 season was a slight improvement on that.

'We've been brilliant in the cups this year. In the FA Cup, we were poor, and we should've won that day,' said McGraa, recalling their home loss to Winsford United in the extra preliminary round. 'The Vase was a different story. We weren't the best but got out of jail in each round. It was enjoyable. The Hebburn game was a simple case of they were the better team than us on the day. They had only conceded one goal all season, so it was difficult to beat them, especially once they went ahead.'

The FA Cup and FA Vase were the competitions every club wanted to play in and win. The Vase offered clubs in Step 9 and below of the pyramid a chance to compete for a trophy while picking up well-needed prize money, and the chance to play at Wembley. The FA Cup didn't necessarily offer this opportunity but gave clubs the chance to play in one of the most famous competitions in the world. They could also pick up prize money along the way and get the chance to test their skills against Football League players (if they reached the first round proper). The league cups, on the other hand, weren't necessarily the main focus of the club. Vauxhall Motors won some games but didn't take the league cups as seriously as they did the other competitions, which certainly cost them early on.

'Our run in the league cup came to an end a lot sooner than the other competitions we were in, but it was something we felt we needed to sacrifice. We had beaten a couple of teams in the leagues above comfortably but didn't take the cups serious enough,' said McGraa.

Prior to competing in the North West Counties League Division One South (Step 6), Vauxhall played in the West Cheshire League (Step 7), finishing second to South Liverpool in the 2017/18 season. That was an improvement on the previous season when they finished eighth in the same division. Ahead of 2018/19, they rejoined the North West Counties League, which they had previously won in 1999/2000. In their first year back in the division, they had narrowly missed out on promotion to the Premier Division after Warrington Rylands won the title, but McGraa knew the club were a project in the making and was confident in his side's ability to win the Division One South title the following season.

'We knew we should've gone up the year before, but we finished second and missed out on points-per-game,' he explained. 'We would've gone up [had their points average been better than other teams across the country] and it was hard to take. We kept the same squad together and added some more quality, so the main aim for us was to win the league. We weren't expecting to struggle with promotion.'

Along with the league champions, a select few of the runners-up would get promoted based on their point averages, compared to the leagues at the same level. For the Motormen, an average of just over two points per game was not enough to get promoted ahead of others at their level.

Having played 31 league games during 2019/20, Vauxhall had found themselves 16 points clear at the top, ahead of second-placed FC Oswestry Town. McGraa knew he had to give his players a target in order to keep them motivated for the remainder of the season. The easiest choice for him was a points total. Although they could still be caught by the teams below them having more games to play, the confidence was visible.

'I think it [the league] was done. The main aim for us was getting over 100 points. We only lost three games all season, so the league was done and so was promotion. The goal for us, to keep the players focused on the remainder of the season, was to achieve that points total. We could have got 103 in the end.'

With nothing he could do about the FA's decision, McGraa looked ahead to the next campaign. He knew that he and his squad would have to try and achieve the same feat again, but he also understood that nothing was ever easy. With few opportunities available for promotion, other sides would look to strengthen while he and his coaches had to get themselves focused before they could try and help the players.

'We need to get focused ourselves as a management team and try to change things. The players will get bored of the same routine, and we've got to try and bring in fresh faces to give those players that are here a kick up the backside,' McGraa explained. 'I think pre-season will be hard. The lads will be deflated and it's going to be tough. I'm not looking forward to it.'

When the new season had come around, the mood hadn't changed. For the Motormen, the excitement was lacking, and McGraa still wasn't looking forward to another season in North West Counties League Division One South. It was difficult to get his mind set on a new season, knowing he should have been preparing to manage a Step 5 side, but instead, he wasn't.

'It was hard,' he explained with a sombre voice. 'As expected, we had lost a few players to other sides and we tried to rebuild once again, but the motivation [to go again] wasn't there.'

After a pre-season that seemed to drag on forever, Vauxhall finally began their season on Saturday, 3 October 2020 as they welcomed Stone Old Alleynians to Rivacre Park. The Motormen knew they needed to make a good start to the campaign and the first game was a comfortable 4-1 win over one of their title rivals. The season had barely any time to warm up before McGraa's men were ahead; Michael Burkey made the most of a defensive mistake from the visitors and fired them ahead, before that start was bettered with another goal in the seventh minute, this time when Ben Holmes lifted the ball over the stranded keeper. A further two goals, a spot-kick from 12 yards converted by Glenn Rule and a home debut goal from Noah Robson four minutes from time, either side of a goal for Liam Hickson, gave those on the outside an impression of what they could expect from Vauxhall.

The club played a further six games through October as they remained unbeaten. Two wins against Maine Road as well as victories over Sandbach United, Abbey Hutton United and Alsager Town and a draw at home against Barnton put them top of the table with 19 points. Despite the bright start to the 2020/21 season, the Motormen found themselves holding a narrow lead over Wythenshawe Town who had remained unbeaten themselves, winning six out of six.

'We were still winning games, but we weren't playing our best football,' McGraa said as he looked back on an unusually short season. 'We just got by, but that was enough to win games and grind out results. We still had plenty of games to play and that included both games against Wythenshawe and I was confident we would have beaten them.'

The season hadn't been straightforward up to that point. More restrictions across the country had brought football to a standstill and after 35 days without a game following their 3-1 victory over Maine Road at the end of October, Vauxhall had returned at the start of December for some action in the FA Vase with a 240-mile round trip to Cumbria in the second round of the competition to face Holker Old Boys. The game produced little between the sides as a Ben Holmes goal in the 16th minute was enough to see Vauxhall through to the third round, where they came up against a familiar opponent.

After an additional fortnight without competitive action, McGraa led his side out at the Hebburn Sports & Social Ground against Hebburn Town who, at the time of competing in the 2020/21 edition of the Vase, were still awaiting their date at Wembley for the 2019/20 final.

The third-round tie was an entertaining affair between the two sides, who were leading their respective divisions; the Motormen sat top of North West Counties League Division One South while the Hornets were sitting pretty at the top of Northern League Division One. Hebburn had taken the lead in the 16th minute as Michael McKeown fired an effort beyond the keeper after latching on to a loose ball in the box, and that lead was held for much of the match, with both sides having several opportunities. That was until Hayden Cooper found an equaliser with 15 minutes left. The midfielder latched on to a low cross and tapped the ball home.

The tide seemed to have turned in the 90th minute as Vauxhall took the lead. Michael Burkley skipped his way through the defensive line, unleashing a shot that found the back of the net, but four minutes seemed too long for the visitors as Hebburn found their equaliser in the third minute of the time allocated. The Hornets needed a goal and found one after throwing the kitchen sink at the Vauxhall goal, a cross from Dan Groves nestling itself in the far corner. With the sides level at the blow of the referee's whistle, the game was settled on penalties. Hebburn converted all of their penalties to seal a 5-3 win after Vauxhall had missed their fourth.

McGraa said, 'After the lengthy break, we returned to action in the Vase. We had progressed through one round, but narrowly lost to Hebburn. I think we had played well in that game and were unlucky to have lost it on penalties against a side who had made it to Wembley. We couldn't dwell on that game though; we were told by the league that [our game on Boxing Day] would possibly be our last game, so we knew it was coming.'

The match against Cammell Laird on Boxing Day had kept Vauxhall above Wythenshawe Town by a point. Forbes and Smyth had given Vauxhall a 2-0 lead but it wasn't a comfortable win. The visitors had pulled one back in the 73rd minute through an own goal, but it wasn't enough to halt their progress. It was the seventh win of the season, giving them 22 points, but in the back of their minds they knew football would be halted for the foreseeable. With that in mind, it made it tough to plan for McGraa for any possible return to action.

'It was [tough], more so for the lads than it was for me. It was hard for them to get their fitness levels right because of the uncertainty around whether we'd play with all the restrictions. We started the season a lot later than expected, returned around Christmas time following a lengthy break before going into the new year without any football. We were trying to avoid injuries and that made it hard as well,' McGraa said.

The decision by the Government to put the country into a third national lockdown stifled any hope of the players returning for the remainder of the season. That left problems for both the clubs and the Football Association. The 2019/20 season had seen near on 80 per cent of the games being played, but it was declared null and void, so it was difficult to see how less than 25 per cent of a campaign would result in anything different. You couldn't blame clubs for fearing that the season would have just been declared null and void again.

It was late evening on Wednesday, 24 February when the FA called time on 2020/21. In an official statement by the governing body, they announced that after considering the data they had gathered from across the National League System, it was agreed that the season would be curtailed, but the results would not be expunged. Submissions on the decision were made by 99.1 per cent of Step 3 and 4 clubs and 95.8 per cent of clubs at Steps 5 and 6, with over 76 per cent of all those clubs voting for the season to be cut short.

With no decision on what would follow the curtailment, the FA knew that they would have to revisit the discussion of restructure of the National League System. With that came 'Project Non-League', a proposal from non-league clubs to the FA for the restructure of the lower tiers to go ahead, rewarding the strongest sides over the course of two seasons without the fear of relegation. That campaign certainly affected Vauxhall Motors who, having collected 104 points from 39 games across the two curtailed seasons, sat top of the North West Counties League Division One South combined season table with 2.66 points per game. That saw them sit 0.40 PPG ahead of Wythenshawe Town, putting them in pole position for promotion to the Premier Division.

'When the second season was curtailed, I thought it was going to be a repeat of the first. I didn't think for one second that we would get promoted. I really didn't,' said McGraa.

The announcement of Vauxhall's promotion came on Tuesday, 18 March as the Football Association disclosed the 107 clubs that would be upwardly moved within Steps 4 to 6. The Motormen were joined by second-placed Wythenshawe Town in the Premier Division, while Stone Old Alleynians were also promoted, moving to the Midlands Football League Premier Division. With the promotion came a new challenge for McGraa and he knew exactly what he wanted to achieve in the next chapter of the club's history.

'We want to challenge, but we've got to be realistic as a club. We are not ready to go and challenge the top teams, but next season will be about familiarising ourselves with the league before having a good go the following season.

'I'm looking forward to facing all of them [the sides in the Premier Division]. The league is something new to us. Everyone's going to be talking about the Macclesfield games, home and away, as it's surely going to be a big crowd. Some players won't ever get the chance to play in front of crowds like that again, so that's the standout game. I'm looking forward to going head-to-head with all the teams and seeing if we can compete at the level we are at now.'

* * *

Ware Football Club didn't sit top of the league by a substantial number of points, leading Hanwell Town by six, but they weren't content with the null and void decision. Although they had played two, three and even four games more than the teams below, manager Paul Halsey felt his side would have still lifted the Isthmian League South Central title, had they been allowed to continue.

'Our next game was Hanwell at home,' he said. 'I felt we were confident going into the game and that we could revenge the 1-0 loss at their place with a win ourselves. I felt that if we had won that game, we would have gone on to win the league.'

A win over the Geordies would have given Ware a nine-point lead and even if Hanwell had won their two games in hand, the Blues would have remained ahead of their title rivals and in control going towards the end of the season. The run-in for Halsey and his side would have been tough, leading up to Bracknell on the final day, a team just outside the play-offs themselves, but looking at the other sides in and around the play-offs Ware were still confident they would finish at the summit.

Halsey said, 'The teams below us all had a tough run-in too. We had Hanwell and Westfield at home, while also needing to travel away to Barking, Waltham Abbey, Chipstead and Bracknell Town, who were all within the top ten. I felt had we beaten Hanwell and Westfield at home, we would have been in a better position because the teams chasing us had each other to play, so they were all going to drop points.'

When the season was voided, Hanwell, Uxbridge, Chertsey Town, and Westfield occupied the play-off places, with Bracknell and Waltham Abbey both sitting two points off the final spot. They had all played fewer games than Ware, but the Blues sat 12 points ahead of fifth-placed Westfield.

The 2019/20 season had been a stark improvement on the previous campaign. That had been Halsey's first campaign in charge of Ware, and he was quietly pleased with finishing seventh. Although they had begun with a win over South Park at home, two losses against Westfield and Cheshunt had made for a difficult start. September had made for better reading. A draw and a defeat were followed by a four-game unbeaten run before they faced back-to-back defeats again, losing 3-0 to Hanwell and 3-1 to Hayes & Yeading United.

Halsey led his players on a six-game unbeaten run between November and December before a narrow loss to Cheshunt brought that to an end. A further three wins briefly boosted their cause – to finish as high as possible – before Northwood inflicted their seventh loss of the season. The new year had brought new sense of joy to the club as the Blues were defeated just once in 11 games by eventual champions Hayes & Yeading before April had proven tough for them. Three losses and two wins ended the 2018/19 season in that final month and, looking back, it was clear to see that a winning run in April could have propelled the club to a play-off place, but it was far from disappointing for Halsey.

'I had taken over a couple of years ago, and in my first season, we had finished in the top half. We felt we had done really well that season and although we fell off towards the end, we felt it was still a good season. I had signed players I felt were going to push us towards the title and that's exactly what happened [the following season].

The team changed quite a bit, but I set out to go and push for the league [title].'

With a decent season behind them, Halsey's mindset turned to being outright winners of the Isthmian League South Central Division ahead of the 2019/20 season.

'We made a bit of a slow start, but we found our feet and were scoring goals for fun. At the start of the last season [2019/20], I had lost players like David Cowley and Brandon Adams, so people were questioning where our goals were going to come from. That just speaks for itself when we went on to score 90 goals in the league. Josh Williams and Dan Rumens were brought in, and I had strengthened where I needed to ahead of the season.'

After an opening-day 3-3 draw against Staines Town, who had just been relegated from the Southern League Premier Division South, Halsey's men extended their unbeaten run by a further nine games that spanned across the first four months of the season. A win against Barking followed before they were held 1-1 by both FC Romania and Chertsey Town. Ware then registered a further four wins, beating Chalfont St Peter, Harlow Town, Uxbridge, and Bedfont Sports, before they were held by South Park at the end of October. A further victory against Northwood was the last of the unbeaten start to as Hanwell Town inflicted the Blues' first defeat of the season.

The narrow 1-0 defeat to the Geordies could have derailed Ware's promotion push, but instead they continued to pick up points. Another 3-3 draw, this time at home to Hertford Town, was followed by 18 goals in three games;

6-1 victories over Chipstead and Bracknell Town as well as a 6-0 win over Ashford Town (Middlesex) had put the club in a commanding position as they sought promotion. The win over Ashford had come at the start of December and, while Ware had only lost one game in the opening four months, they doubled that in December alone. Tooting & Mitcham United and Waltham Abbey had proven tough opposition for the Hertfordshire club as they lost 2-1 and 3-2 respectively, but had picked up wins against Marlow and FC Romania in the games that followed the defeats.

Into the new year, Ware almost saw out the season with an unbeaten final three months. Three wins against Chertsey Town, Bedfont Sports and South Park weren't enough for a perfect January as they had been beaten 4-0 by Westfield, but still, Halsey's men pushed on towards what they hoped would have been a promotion to cap off a great season. February had been the month with most games – six – but that didn't cause too many problems for Ware as they dropped just four points. A draw against Uxbridge was followed by victories over Harlow, Ashford, Tooting & Mitcham and Northwood, before they drew against Marlow at the end of the month. That was followed by what would be the final game, a 3-1 win over Hertford, on Saturday, 7 March 2020. The club had capped off another nine-game unbeaten run, leaving them top by six points.

The players' boots were still warm from the premature final game of 2019/20 when the decision to bring an end to the season was finalised. In a single decision, a season of hard work and enjoyment was ended and the FA's ruling frustrated Halsey.

'It's no secret how I feel about the decision,' he exclaimed. 'It was a rash decision as we were one of the first leagues to come to that decision. From the FA, right down to our league and below, it was a poor decision, and I don't think they took everything into consideration. They didn't need to make the decision so early. I felt they should have let it settle down and reassess where we were in June. We could have finished the season.'

If the lower leagues had their season ended briskly, Halsey felt the 'elite' leagues should have followed. He felt the choices those competitions got should have been applied to Steps 3 to 6, and as he thought back to March 2020, he had his own solution for how the season could have ended.

'My second option was to not start the [2020/21] season until the suspended season had finished. We had played close to 80 per cent of our games, and already this season, we have played seven or eight games, which could have been the rest of last season. To see the National League going on a points-per-game basis, I felt it was disgraceful the way they [the FA] dealt with it. We could have finished the season in place of the start of the new season [in September] and started the 2020/21 season after Christmas. That meant the season would have finished later, but it would have been finished. There are plenty of people that would agree that null and voiding the season was too easy of a decision and the only sides that didn't agree with it were those fighting relegation.'

He paused, and added, 'It just made a mockery of the system.'

The new season began in September, a month later than originally scheduled, so focus immediately turned to the opening game. Halsey still had ambitions to win the title and, although teams who had struggled or were off the pace would have strengthened their squads, he felt his side would go on to to challenge once again.

'I'm not going to change my mindset or plans,' he explained. 'The minimum is always going to be the play-offs, but I want to win that league. We expected a lot of clubs to go out and strengthen, but I felt the money situation [that came with the lost revenue] would have been a problem for everyone. It seemed to be the opposite and more had more money which would make the season more competitive.'

While several managers weren't looking forward to the new season and having to motivate their players, it was a different story for Halsey. A simple chat with all his players proved they were ready for another season and ready to battle again.

'Some of the players at the club aren't getting any younger and a few of them were planning to win the league and hang up their boots. I spoke to a lot of them [through the summer] and let's be clear, everyone at the club, from the chairman to the fans, was absolutely gutted with the outcome. I knew I would have to try and find a way to motivate them, but I didn't need to. Every phone call I made came back with the same response. They all told me they had unfinished business and a lot of those who planned to retire weren't going to until we had won the title. For me as a manager, that was phenomenal and simply magic. It was easy for them to walk away, but I have a great bunch of players who play for me, and they are all friends, so they aren't just players of the club.'

There was a huge contrast between how Halsey had seen the 2019/20 and 2020/21 seasons. The former had been one of his best as a manager and, although it was not concluded how he had hoped, he would still have fond memories and would look back at it along with his time at Hertford, but the latter wasn't going to be firm in Halsey's memory as a great one.

'As a manager, it was one of my best seasons. I had some great times with Hertford and with their fans but building something special at Ware has been great. I'm a Ware man myself and live opposite the ground. We aren't just bringing players to the club, but we are also attracting fans, through the gate and all the local people are interested in what we are doing.'

There was still uncertainty around whether or not the season would be played. The country had been in lockdown since March 2020 and in order to even get the season started, the Government would have had to ease restrictions, allowing fans to attend matches. It was a huge ask from those at the top, but it had to be done in order for the lower leagues to survive. Those restrictions were slightly eased in May, around seven weeks after they were enforced, as the Government allowed for a 15 per cent capacity at grounds initially before taking that up to 30 per cent.

'I think everyone was quite pleased that we had come out of the lockdown, but like most people, we were concerned we would face another one. We were still a little disappointed with the outcome of the previous season as we felt we had a good side, but there wasn't anything we could do about that,' Halsey said.

The 2020/21 season had begun on Saturday, 19 September as the Blues made the trip to Wheatsheaf Park to face Staines Town. It hadn't been the first competitive game of that season, though, as they had already eased past Step 5 Southend Manor at Southchurch Park in the FA Cup. They had bowed out of the competition a week before their league campaign got under way as they lost 2-0 to Canvey Island, who went on to reach the second round proper and lost to National League side Boreham Wood.

The opening game was a defeat for Halsey's men. After finding themselves leading 2-1 in the 25th minute with goals from Louis Rose and Liam Hope, the visitors failed to make that count as two goals in quick succession sealed a 3-2 win for Staines. The loss was nothing more than a bump in the road as the Blues won their next two games.

'It wasn't a worry at all,' said Halsey. 'With Staines, they were a young side with a new manager. I was more concerned with the chances we missed and the goals that we conceded. All three goals were things we could deal with on the training pitch, but I wasn't concerned we would go on a bad run. I never go by the first game because you've always got a whole season to catch that up. Nothing really changed with the tactics or my philosophy [to get the first win of the season]. The new players who had come in had to buy into that, and it took a few games for them to adapt.'

Wins against Bedfont Sports and Chalfont St Peter had looked to get Ware going on a good run of form, but they couldn't capitalise as they faced another setback with their second defeat in four games, losing to Uxbridge. They had taken the lead through Dan Rumens in the 23rd minute but an 11-minute spell just before half-time had given the Reds the advantage, with neither team scoring in the second half. For Halsey, it was another game where he felt the club had contributed to their own fall.

'If you look at the Uxbridge and Staines games, they were very similar in the way that we made mistakes we shouldn't have made. I think we rightly lost that 2-1, but it could have easily been the other way around. I feel we could have dealt with the forward play a lot better. We couldn't afford to lose too many games, so we worked hard on the training ground and went on a short winning run.'

Work on the training ground was exactly what Ware needed as they won their next three games. The first had seen Halsey's side beat Barking at home. Leigh Rose had given them the lead in the 27th minute before the visitors found a leveller just ten minutes later. Ware had looked to avoid a repeat of the Uxbridge game, and goals from Marcus Milner a couple of minutes into the second half and Reece Crowter 20 minutes from time ensured they got the three points over the line. That victory had been followed by wins over South Park and Harlow Town, putting Ware third and a point off the sides above with a game in hand. For Ware, it was the last time they played in 2020/21.

Their Tuesday night game against Harlow had been watched by 249 people as Ware eased to a 6-1 victory over the Hawks, but there was some anticipation in the air regarding what could happen if the pandemic continued to worsen at the rate it was. That fear was realised on Saturday, 31 October as the Government announced a second national lockdown to combat the ongoing surge.

Halsey said, 'As the season went on, I think we all knew it was heading for a lockdown. We were hoping it wouldn't go that way, but realistically, we were concerned it would. It was certainly a downer that that had happened as it had a knock-on effect throughout the club, but again, what could we do about it?'

While another lockdown had dampened the spirits of those in and around the club, no one had expected to not play another game. After four weeks the lockdown had come to an end, but no football was then played before the third national lockdown, enforced in January, confirmed the fears of many, with no more league fixtures scheduled during the 2020/21 season. Thoughts of managers and players alike had turned to what would be the outcome of the decision, with a sense of impending déjà vu, but for Halsey, he didn't feel enough games had been played to worry about the outcome of the season.

'We didn't feel the season would go the same way as the previous season because we hadn't played the same number of games. I don't think there was a sense of déjà vu, but

I feel it [curtailing the season] was the right thing to do. Although I found it strange that they null and voided one, but just curtailed the other and used points-per-game to decide promotion.'

The FA had made a decision to promote sides from Steps 5 and 6, meaning Ware had missed out on the chance to be promoted on points-per-game. Instead, when the FA announced the constitution for 2021/22, they had been moved laterally from Isthmian League South Central Division to Southern League Division One Central. It hadn't been the news they were hoping for, but it gave the club a new challenge to look forward to rather than the disappointment of facing the same sides in the same league. It was a completely new division though, with FC Romania, Hertford Town, Waltham Abbey, and Harlow joining them from the Isthmian League. That gave Halsey a good balance of familiarity and the unknown, which made for an exciting season ahead.

'Whatever league it is, I will be exactly the same. I set out to go and win that league, but now, we will face a number of new teams that we don't know. It's definitely going to be an interesting season. A few sides were moved across the Isthmian League alongside us, so I will be looking forward to those games, but I will also be looking forward to visiting the new grounds too. I'm not disappointed by the decision [not to promote clubs to Step 3], I'm just excited for the new challenge.'

* * *

If it was a difficult time for clubs, it was even harder for those whose job it was to make the news clear for everyone and explain what was going on. The media had to make sense of it all and, as the presenter of the *Non-League Show*, Ollie Bayliss found himself at the heart of the coverage. The communication and information between the FA and individual leagues were scarce and brief, but people were seeking answers. Bayliss used his presence on Twitter to filter and share information, explaining it in layman's terms.

He said, 'It's a really difficult time for everybody. I don't envy the position the decision-makers are in. There is no right answer or easy option for those who run the leagues and for the FA. They've been forced to make one of the most difficult decisions they will ever make in football administration, and they have to make it without being face-to-face. On top of that, several key figures are fighting the virus themselves and are unwell. Clearly the health of the people is more important than football right now.'

It begged the question as to whether the pressure that the authorities were under had contributed to the haste with which some of the decisions were made. Through the frustration, it was hard not to question whether that affected the decision, especially with some officials being ill. Was everyone present?

'For me, the leagues and the FA have made the wrong decision. I think it was a decision that was made too early. We were still in March and only two weeks into the suspension of games when time was called on Steps 3 to 7,' explained Bayliss. 'I would have liked to see teams that occupied the automatic promotion spots on their current points-per-game averages promoted. I think they could have promoted with no relegations. With the expansion of the leagues in non-league, along with clubs who will inevitably withdraw, I think the numbers would have pretty much worked. It's also a method that could have been applied throughout the English football pyramid without many feeling the decision was unfair.'

The FA didn't agree. For them, their primary concern was the safety of everyone involved in the sport and the FA's head of the National League System had put out a statement explaining the association's decision not to allow for promotion and relegation at those levels.

'The truth is that the consequence of clubs being promoted is that others will need to be relegated. The application of a points-per-game model would result in certain clubs that currently sit above the relegation zone falling into those places. Equally, there would be certain clubs that currently sit in a play-off position that would not qualify as a result of the points-per-game model. This model also doesn't address the issue of how to deal with the play-off matches and how to identify a winner who would consequently benefit from promotion.'

The decision from the FA was never going to please everyone, but the clubs missing out on promotion felt that clubs in the relegation places were benefiting more from the decision. The FA already had plans in the works to expand the non-league pyramid at the end of the 2019/20 season. The idea was a restructuring of the league borders along with adding another division at Step 4 to address the travelling of clubs between the north-east and Peterborough. They also wanted to increase Step 5 by two divisions, taking it up to 16, and reduce Step 6 by three, taking it down to 17. A restructure of the pyramid meant that clubs could be promoted based on points-per-game across the country, like it had been planned to happen, but the decision was made to delay the restructure until the end of the 2020/21 season at the earliest.

Bayliss said, 'The best solution would have been to promote teams without relegation with points-per-game. Relegating teams on points-per-game is particularly harsh, especially if it's by a narrow margin. The FA's decision affected around 100 leagues from Step 3 to 7. There shouldn't have been a strict "one size fits all" rule. Non-league is used to seeing clubs being promoted on ground-grading, sideways movement, and reprieves. I think teams could have got on board with some promotions, but no relegations.'

Justifying the comparative difference between the way the FA saw the Football League and the lower leagues made it far tougher for Bayliss and his fellow reporters. The Premier League, EFL and National League were offered the chance to continue when it was safe to do so, but again, it was difficult not to question the decision. The thoughts of those who weren't able to continue were that non-league and grassroots football had been thrown to the gutter. The clubs that had everything to lose wanted to continue, and would have been happy to wait as long as was needed, but they weren't given the chance. Despite this, Bayliss understood that far more clubs supported the curtailment of the season.

'Many clubs did mostly support the season being finished. Leagues did consult with clubs and the majority wanted confirmation that games had finished for the season. Having some certainty allows clubs to financially plan and sort out contracts. For many non-league players, they were on weekly contracts until May and clubs were worried they would have had to extend them without knowing if games would be played.'

The National League already had a longer process to decide the outcome of the season. After a majority vote to abandon what remained of 2020/21, the league issued a vote to decide the outcome of promotions and relegations, but this was never an option for the lower tiers. Instead, the FA expunged the results, wiping any trace of the season from their records.

'We are seeing a number of unhappy clubs being vocal about the decision to expunge the leagues. It will be sure to mean many clubs will withdraw or fold over the season and the financial impact of the current crisis will see a much greater number sadly leave the pyramid. It's very hard for the FA to look after all of the several thousand teams who play lower-league football, but there hasn't been much in the way of grants and support being offered to these clubs,' explained Bayliss.

The option of using points-per-game may have changed the course of who would have been promoted or relegated and while the majority of clubs in promotion places would have achieved the same on PPG, Bayliss understood how hard it was on the clubs affected. Saffron Walden Town sat top of the Essex Senior League when the season was voided, but both Walthamstow and Hashtag United were within three points and had three games in hand each. A PPG solution would have seen them miss out on promotion to Step 4, but unlike the Bloods, clubs like Worthing and Colney Heath would have achieved their destiny whether the season had been played or not. Still, the thoughts were mainly focused on the clubs who had already achieved that, with games spare.

'The decision was particularly harsh on Vauxhall [Motors] and Jersey [Bulls]. They had already celebrated promotion. The Bulls had a 100 per cent record and hadn't dropped a single point in their 27 games, so these clubs just showed why I felt teams in automatic promotion positions should have been promoted,' suggested Bayliss. 'It doesn't really do anyone any favours having them compete at Step 6 again, but I'm sure both will have a good campaign. It'll be hard to motivate themselves to go again.'

The words of Bayliss echoed those of Vauxhall's manager Mike McGraa. The question of where the motivation would come from certainly would spring up again. The players were looking forward to a new challenge; instead they were set to face an even tougher season for the wrong reasons. The clubs that led in the North West Counties League would certainly improve their squads, hoping they'd be one of the four teams to achieve promotion.

Another issue with promotion was that the PPG solution didn't take into consideration the teams who had started to pick up some form. For them, deciding a season on point averages was not fair.

The heartfelt sympathies also went out to those who were close to achieving the same feat but would still need points from their remaining games to seal their fate. South Shields, Maldon & Tiptree and Stowmarket Town held substantial leads in their respective leagues. Maldon & Tiptree sat 13 points clear at the top of the Isthmian League North Division but had four games in hand over second-placed Bury Town due to their excellent FA Cup run, while South Shields were comfortably ahead of FC United of Manchester in the Norther Premier League. Elsewhere, Stowmarket were well ahead in the Eastern Counties League Premier Division, holding a 15-point lead over both Norwich United and Stanway Rovers. They weren't the only sides to be sat at the top of their respective leagues and denied the chance of promotion, but it showed what the FA needed to consider when voiding the season.

Bayliss said, 'Clubs will be playing the same clubs in the same division despite having a good campaign. By the time we kick off next season, it will have been at least five months since football was last played, but the boost in excitement and support upon the return of football will hopefully help keep teams motivated in the early months at least.

'Players, managers and volunteers have worked hard to get themselves in a good position at the top of the table. Clubs have spent a lot of money to chase promotion and sponsors have paid into a project. No one has seen a reward for their efforts or their finances, so sponsors could justifiably walk away next season, as could players and managers. Teams who have had a good season this year might not necessarily be able to have a good campaign next time.'

A gambling company were one of the sponsors that made the decision to pull out of their deal following the end of the 2019/20 season. They had sponsored the Isthmian League but felt their contract couldn't be honoured despite having a year left, while they made it clear it didn't have anything to do with the ongoing pandemic. Despite that, for the league itself, it made it tougher to find a sponsorship as the economy had already taken a hit, but they were keen to continue their relationship with sponsors.

A league statement read, 'We are very disappointed that this decision has been made as it means that we are not able to develop the relationship with the sponsor. We are actively looking for a new sponsor, but we are apprehensive at this time due to the general economic downturn due to Covid-19. We believe we have a good and marketable product which has attracted sponsors for nearly 40 years, and we hope will continue to do so once we are able to restart the league.'

The financial impact on clubs and the lower leagues was the toughest part of the decisions, but there was nothing that could be done. With sponsors pulled away from their respective sponsees and the 2019/20 season ceasing to exist, all people could do was look back at what could have been.

Bayliss said, 'It was particularly harsh [the decision to expunge the season] given the efforts and achievements of so many clubs. When the Second World War disrupted football 80 years ago, the leagues were simply left unfinished. That would have been kinder and fairer. Perhaps there were legal reasons why they needed to expunge the season rather than just indefinitely suspend the season. I'd have preferred clubs to have been rewarded for their efforts for the part of the season that was played.'

There was plenty of optimism as 2020/21 approached, with clubs and supporters hoping the new season would be free from disruption and completed in full after the first unprecedented season had come to an end. Many didn't want to think ahead to what might happen if the pandemic took hold again, but the majority were just excited to get back through the turnstiles and into grounds around the country ahead of what was set to be an exciting season after a lengthy break.

'I think when we started the 2020/21 season in September, there was a lot of optimism. There wasn't yet much evidence of a second or third wave [of coronavirus]. Maybe the FA should have put something in the rules to dictate what happened if the season was curtailed, but I don't think it was unreasonable to start the season as normal,' said Bayliss.

The new season had merely been two months old when the second lockdown was brought into force at the start of

November, but there was still hope that overall it would largely be unaffected by the goings-on around the country. That break lasted for four weeks before football was able to resume with a few games before the non-league world would fall silent for the annual Christmas break, but new restrictions days before the festive period squandered any plans to return in the new year to continue the season. Although it looked set to be the end of a second season earlier than expected, the same sense of disappointment wasn't replicated from 2019/20.

'I think there was a bit more of a feeling of inevitability about the season stopping in December. Fewer games had been played than the previous season, so I think most clubs were resigned to losing another season to Covid. There was less anger than the season before,' said Bayliss.

The talk of 'Project Non-League' had been around since the start of the year as many suspected the season wouldn't be finished following the lockdown in January 2021. The proposal behind the idea was that clubs would be promoted based on the two incomplete seasons to fill in gaps left by those who had left the pyramid and the imminent restructure to the lower levels by the FA. While it was a good idea for most leagues, the FA only had plans to fill Step 4 and below, meaning clubs looking to get promoted to Step 3 and above wouldn't have got their just reward, despite also being affected by the restructure. For Bayliss, the governing body had made a huge error in not applying the project to all the divisions, as he felt the pyramid needed promotion at all levels to happen.

'Broadly the suggestion from "Project Non-League" was adapted, although there were some significant differences. It was only used to form new leagues, so just teams at Steps 5 to 7 were promoted. It means gaps still exist in leagues and it's not clear why the FA didn't take the opportunity to fill all the gaps.

'Clubs at Steps 3 and 4 have every right to be frustrated that they weren't elevated. There were gaps at Step 3 and 4 that could have been filled. The aim is for Step 2 leagues to run at 24 clubs, so there's scope for seven clubs to be moved up to that level, but in reality, I think every top-placed club that wanted promotion was given it. In many cases at Step 6, leagues promoted up to three clubs. That was to fill the new leagues at Step 5, but there's a slight bias towards clubs being promoted to Step 4 in the north, because the new league that's added is in the Northern Premier League. This situation was communicated to clubs ahead of the season.'

The restructure had gone ahead as planned ahead of 2021/22 as the FA added another league at Step 4, a further two at Step 5 and reduced Step 6 by three. While that had gone ahead as planned, Bayliss understood that the FA had found themselves in a difficult position, despite also giving 110 clubs upward movement.

'It's a really difficult job for the FA who get a list of clubs in each step and have to sort them into geographic leagues. Clubs understandably get frustrated, especially when they get moved around regularly. It affects their playing squad and sponsorships as well as travel times. There's no easy solution to this situation, however.'

The 2021/22 campaign was set to be huge for the lower leagues. After two years without a full season and promotion based on points-per-game to fill in gaps for a restructure, it was paramount that clubs needed a full season behind them and promotion and relegation to return to a sense of normality. Whether that was going to happen would remain to be seen.

Bayliss said, 'Promotion and relegation will hopefully be back to something close to normal. However, we will still have significant gaps in the pyramid. The National League North and South aim to increase their numbers to 24, so we'll need more promotion places and fewer relegation spots for a season or two at least. I also think it's crucial we get a full season in. Clubs, players, and fans are getting increasingly frustrated by the situation. We risk losing a generation in the lower-league game and clubs rely on the finances from fans, so it's crucial we get them back as normal and as soon as possible.'

2

Dark Times

WALTHAMSTOW CAME third in 2018/19, a fantastic achievement for a club that had previously fought relegation. Despite winning 11 of their final 13 games, Stow missed out on second by two points and automatic promotion by seven points. The team could be proud of what they achieved under the management of Ryan Maxwell, especially with the run of 11 wins, but the loss to Sporting Bengal United certainly derailed their cause. They had given themselves too much to do towards the end of the season. By January, they had already drawn seven and lost four of their 20 games, but they improved over the last four months. Between January and April, Stow had played 18 games. Fourteen of their 24 wins during 2018/19 had come in those last four months, with Stow also facing three defeats and drawing one. The target for the following season was crystal clear: improvement.

Stow had found themselves in a near-death experience once again as they battled to survive in the Essex Senior

League. Then named Waltham Forest FC, they were scrapping at the wrong end of the table during the 2017/18 season.

'While we've only been relegated a few times in our long history, we've been through quite a few relegation battles, especially recently,' said Walthamstow's communications manager, Andrzej Perkins. 'The non-league game isn't as popular as it once was, especially in east London. While village clubs have flourished, we've struggled. The last couple of seasons have been really enjoyable because we're growing as a club and looking towards the top of the table rather than the bottom.'

The struggles didn't just happen on the pitch, but off it too. Following factors beyond their control, the club had found it tough. As 2017 drew to a close, the situation at Forest was looking bleak with a near-empty donations bucket being passed around an equally deserted ground. The team was unrecognisable from one week to the next and it all seemed to be a case of enjoying it while it lasted.

'We were in a position where we couldn't pay any expenses for players, and a manager who was using the team as a shop window for players to get trials at higher clubs. That part worked okay; players like Mo Sagaf and Muhammed Faal are now playing professionally,' Perkins explained, 'but the majority didn't stick around long enough in the first team to have any sort of team spirit. It felt like we were watching 11 separate players rather than a team who were all together.

'In 2017, our chairman Turgut Esendagli sadly passed away and we were only a few days away from folding completely. We organised a fundraising match and did some other bits which gave us just enough to keep ticking over. Our chairman, Andy Perkins, found a way of saving the club – not for the first time. Eventually we found a way to get through and now we're enjoying the benefits of that dedication.'

The run-in towards the end of the 2017/18 season saw Waltham Forest pick up 11 points from their final five games, having won just two points in the seven games that preceded. Wins against Basildon United, Stansted and Ilford and draws against Redbridge and Southend Manor saw Waltham Forest finish 17th in the Essex Senior League and avoid relegation, but for those at the club, it was a chance to have a breather before preparing for the new season.

'It [avoiding relegation] felt more of a relief than a celebration,' said Perkins. 'We played Ilford on the last day of the season, knowing a win would keep us up. They had our former striker Billy Cove, in goal, so the game was a bit of an anticlimax in the end. We knew that having stayed up we were in a really good position to push on the following season.'

Waltham Forest achieved the very win they needed, beating Ilford 3-1 at home. Despite dominating from the off, an early Ilford lead had looked to make it a tough day for Forest as Chris Lockwood made no mistake from the spot, smashing the ball into the roof of the net. But the mood changed among the few home supporters before the half was out as Shomari Barnwell levelled the game from the penalty spot.

Forest came out in the second half knowing what they needed to do. A couple of corners had pressured the Foxes' goal and Josh Brimacombe-Wiard capitalised as he smashed the ball home after it had fallen to him. That goal, together with Rheo Josephs' tap-in at the back post just three minutes later, settled the nerves of the Waltham Forest supporters before the game petered out as both sides enjoyed the end of a tough season.

But while 2017/18 closed with an anticlimactic feeling, it was just what the club needed to push on. With a change of name and Ryan Maxwell continuing as manager, Walthamstow were looking good for the 2018/19 season.

Perkins said, 'I think the biggest changes were behind the scenes. Having stayed up and seen the crowds increase, it gave us all a renewed enthusiasm to really make a go of things. The change of name to Walthamstow was huge and really started to make relationships with the local community.'

The squad continued to grow as Stow settled into a structured unit. Maxwell demanded players to match his own commitment and work ethic on and off the pitch, and always had the time to engage with the fans. The boss had started a game in defensive midfield and could be heard shouting 'Can you do this?' at Gus Douglas, who had been warming the bench for a few matches. Simmering down into his new role as player-manager, he was increasingly aware of the fact that he himself probably wouldn't last for the full 90 minutes, despite arguably being the fittest player on the pitch. Douglas came on and did him proud, never looking back and soon becoming a regular starter. Maxwell knew how to get the most out of his squad and limited himself to cameo appearances in order to concentrate on the bigger picture. It was also no secret he held a reputation and was sometimes out of the squad for disciplinary reasons. He was booked in most games and sent off twice; one red came against Takeley for a bad tackle, and the following Saturday, while suspended from playing, he was sent from the dugout in the FA Cup.

The fortunes of Walthamstow had changed. At the end of 2018/19 Stow had finished third behind Hullbridge Sports and Stansted. Although they had missed out on promotion, it was a vast improvement from what the supporters had seen before. A run of one loss in 14 games, going down 4-1 to Takeley, had made for a good start, but as the season went on Stow failed to hit the same heights, losing six games in total. Walthamstow had embarked on two runs of eight games unbeaten, but that was all they could manage until the end of the season.

The team behind the scenes had made a difference to the improved Walthamstow. Maxwell had used pre-season to sign a host of talented players and put them through their paces. The team settled into a core group and produced some consistently good results, meaning Walthamstow were now operating towards the top of the table rather than the bottom.

The arrival of Dwade James from Leyton Athletic halfway through 2018/19 meant the club and fans were treated to a lot more goals than they'd seen previously. There was also a modest rise in numbers on the terraces, with the locals responding well to the club's name change and personnel.

Perkins said, 'Having the right players makes a huge difference. The state of football in the Essex Senior League means that there's only going to be a few clubs challenging at the top of the table, and in that first season, we had James Pegram then Dwade James smashing in the goals.

'The players were completely different, but it was good to see the same people behind the scenes and in the stands – the ones who had stood by the club through thick and thin. They deserve any success we have now more than anyone. We're building on the history of what was once one of the biggest amateur clubs in the country – we can't forget that when we are trying to push forward.'

The third-place finish saw Walthamstow go into the 2019/20 season as one of the favourites to achieve promotion and win the title. While they had built a strong side under Maxwell, other teams wanted to spoil the party, but no one had anticipated Hashtag United having another good season in only their second as a non-league club, with the likes of Stansted, Takeley, Hadley and Saffron Walden also expected to be fighting at the top of the table.

'It was always going to be difficult,' said Perkins. 'There was little between us, Hashtag United and Saffron Walden. Hadley and Takeley were both impressive too, but even though they faltered towards the end of the season, you couldn't rule them out. Despite being one of the favourites, we only took eight out of the possible 21 points from those other top five sides. That gave us an idea of where we needed to improve next year.'

The 2019/20 title battle had all but become a three-horse race as Saffron Walden, Hashtag and Stow battled for the crown. Hadley would have still considered themselves in the race, only sitting six points off Walthamstow, but the top three sides sat 13, 15 and 16 points ahead of fifth-placed Stansted respectively. Having had a good season previously, Walthamstow were always going to have a target on their backs and that showed when Stansted and Takeley played defensively away from home, trying to draw right from the off or even snatch a late win in the 90th minute at the Lodge. Under Maxwell, Stow had achieved a vital win over Stansted, with Dwade James scoring the only goal of the game, but they suffered a 1-0 defeat at home to Takeley while the game against Saffron Walden at Wadham Lodge ended 0-0, which seemed like two points dropped rather than one gained, especially with the chances Stow had created.

Towards the end of January, a change in management was on the cards. Stow had fought back from 2-0 down to beat Clapton at their temporary home of Southchurch Park in Southend, but that was to be Maxwell's final game in the dugout. The decision to part ways was a mutual decision by both parties and, under the new leadership of Max Mitchell, results in the games with those towards the top changed. A 3-0 win over Takeley and a 2-1 win over Saffron Walden away from home had put Walthamstow in a good position alongside their main title rivals, Hashtag. A depleted side could only manage a draw against Ilford at Cricklefields before Mitchell had been appointed, but under the new manager Stow remained in the title race – to the surprise of their supporters.

Walthamstow's last game before the season was voided was the reverse fixture with Hashtag at Tilbury. It almost didn't go ahead as poor weather meant the referee had made a late decision on the condition of the pitch, but after an inspection it was played. The hosts won 2-1 but the result could have been very different. James had hit the post twice in what felt like the exact same spot and was inches away from adding to the penalty he had dispatched earlier in the game, but goals from Albert Keith and George Smith were enough to see the Tags claim the points. There was an improvement under the new management, but there was still plenty of work to do.

It seemed easy to get supporters down for one game but getting them to return was another challenge the club faced. There was no way of identifying someone as a potential fan as the majority of people had a main club they followed, if they were already football-goers. It seemed Walthamstow had to rely on people getting the buzz off their own accord, with the club seemingly receiving more supporters through the gate when they battled to survive and remain in the Essex Senior League than they did when they were one of the favourites for the title. One group who had cemented their place in the stands at Wadham Lodge were the supporters known as the Waltham Rabble. Adam Jackson-Nocher had become one of the regulars, finding the best way to encourage other fans was to hang out the banners, sing the songs and celebrate in style when the team scored. New followers would instantly recognise the Rabble from the flags hanging over the fences, the constant singing of Walthamstow songs based on a handful of 1980s pop classics, especially when the team was struggling, and the confetti cannons going off after every goal.

'The very first Waltham Forest game I saw was in 2013 with a few mates from five-a-side. It was a fun day out organised by a team-mate who lived in Walthamstow, but I didn't return to Wadham Lodge until moving closer to the area a year or two later,' explained Jackson-Nocher.

'My family are all West Ham supporters, and we had a few season tickets we shared between us since I was a kid. When my grandad couldn't manage the journey anymore – after a lifetime in the same seat at Upton Park – and with all the money involved and the move to the Olympic Stadium on the horizon, I was falling out of love with my team and top-tier football altogether.'

With the thoughts of league football out of the question, Jackson-Nocher felt it was time to follow a team further down the pyramid and he wasn't the only one ready to ditch the glamour of the Premier League to watch non-league football.

'My house-mate at the time was in a similar situation and we decided to find a local non-league club to follow.

The Essex Senior League was being torn apart by Haringey Borough, who were about a 20-minute walk away, or there was the bus ride to Waltham Forest, who were scrapping it towards the bottom end of the table. With claret and blue still coursing through our veins, we chose Forest in a heartbeat.'

It wasn't quite love at first sight, but he was gravitating towards the club one way or another.

'We went to a handful of home games, quietly taking it all in from the main stand while the first-team coach chased his unruly toddler along the terrace, desperately barking instructions at a game he'd seen less of than we had, despite our several trips to the bar upstairs.'

A handful of games had turned into more regular visits for Jackson-Nocher as he moved to the area for reasons other than football, giving him the opportunity to visit the Lodge more often with family and friends.

'I moved to Walthamstow at the start of 2017 and a childhood friend of mine happened to move to Clapton at the same time. We hadn't seen that much of each other over the years and decided that Waltham Forest Football Club home games would be a good opportunity to catch up more regularly. My brother also moved nearby with his partner and their little boy, so the Lodge became a bit of a meeting point for us all.

'For one of the first fixtures of 2018, we decided to catch the midday Premier League kick-off in the pub before heading to Wadham Lodge for the main event. By 3pm, we were plastered, choosing to venture into the terraces behind the opposition keeper for a change of scenery. It wasn't long before we were making up Forest chants on the fly and googling how much a banner might cost.'

Standing behind the opposition keeper during the game became a ritual and it wasn't long before a Twitter account had been set up for the Waltham Rabble. It was run by Jackson-Nocher, but he never saw it as his group, allowing others to join as and when they wanted at Walthamstow games.

'It was never established as such, just a few mates who decided to start cheering the team on after a few too many pints one afternoon, and never looked back. The name only came when I decided to set up a Twitter account after a game in February 2018, wanting in on all the non-league gossip online. One of us offered a tin of beer to a chap who was edging closer to us throughout the first half. It turned out to be legendary non-league commentator Chris Walker. He had been on groundhopping duties that day and instantly took the mantle, pulling new Forest songs out of nowhere and trebling the noise all by himself. We had a great time and kept in touch on Twitter from there.'

The Twitter page became a good place to post photos and videos of the game and to try and encourage locals to join in with the club. They had also got themselves out to the pubs with their new banner during the England World Cup games and also managed to get their 'Gold' rip-off chant going in the back room of The Chequers, a nearby pub, and off into the distance down the high street after closing. Although they were supporters, they acted as far more to the football club.

'It's not a fixed or even remotely organised group – hence the name – and I love it when new faces turn up at the Lodge and slowly gravitate towards us and start joining in. We've also helped the club to gain sponsorship from a handful of local businesses and our club scarf hangs proudly over the bar at the Dog & Duck, just round the corner from the Lodge,' said Jackson-Nocher.

3

Keeping a Foot In

STEVE CASTLE had enjoyed an illustrious career throughout his time playing, having had three different spells at Leyton Orient while also featuring for Plymouth Argyle, Birmingham City, Gillingham, Peterborough United and Stevenage.

'I had a very enjoyable career. It's been a while since I've packed it in, and the game has changed since I last played, but while it hasn't changed dramatically, it was about the camaraderie you got with being with the same group of players for a whole season and all having a joint goal – that goal being success. Whether that's individual or collective success, it just couldn't be beaten. Any sport that you can get paid for as a professional is a privilege and I'm grateful for what happened in my playing career.'

His time playing had brought him some joy, but it was clear he had a better time at certain clubs. When it came to choosing a favourite, he had a couple of memories in mind.

'I'm going to be greedy. I was extremely fortunate, and I was at some fantastic football clubs throughout my career. I didn't hit the heights with one or two but in general, I would say the duration of being at Leyton Orient was very satisfying,' he recalled as he looked back fondly on his career. 'With me being captain and it being my local side along with West Ham, it was definitely a highlight. I can't forget my spell at Plymouth either. I spent three years down there as a club captain and scored 40 goals in 100 games, so that was a personal highlight.'

With plenty of memories to look upon, Castle reflected more deeply at his career.

'As a goalscoring midfielder, my hat-trick for both Orient and Plymouth [with one being in the space of six minutes] has to be a highlight. I remember fondly getting promoted with Peterborough at Wembley and that would be another. I can look back with pride on those memories as well as my first promotion with Orient.'

Castle's professional playing career came to an end when he left Stevenage in 2002 but he wanted to keep playing. Having taken some advice, he made the step down the pyramid, joining St Albans City in the Isthmian League.

'As you get older, it becomes a young man's sport. Your body starts to take its toll and I was told by an incredibly good surgeon that my body wouldn't take full-time football anymore. At the age of 37 or 38, I probably wasn't good enough to stay in professional football anyway. I wanted to get into coaching, but it didn't quite happen in that respect. I got asked to go over to St Albans as a player. I already knew two or three of the players and it was quite a fleeting time. I did a full pre-season with no thought of being a coach or a manager but that came very quickly. I just thought I would carry on playing whilst paying a bill or two.'

As a player, he had fallen just short of 50 appearances in the league for St Albans over a two-year spell, but it wasn't just another club. Castle certainly liked non-league and had huge respect for those who already played at that level. This was his opportunity to get involved. He was a professional who didn't mind dropping down the levels to work for his first opportunity in management, even if he had a spell as a player first. His time in non-league had been a step in the right direction towards what he wanted to achieve in football, and he knew it was only the start of his continued journey.

'I think for a lot of people with a professional head on, it's a stepping stone. It's what you would class as proper football. The dedication needed to be a non-league footballer or manager, whilst doing a full-time job, is extremely hard. It's not for all ex-professionals. I know some who wouldn't go anywhere near non-league, but I've got an awful lot of respect for those who are involved. The fact they get themselves extremely fit and have the dedication to do what they do, at a high level, and to have a full-time life outside of football is an incredible achievement.'

While the coaching and management side of his career hadn't started off the way Castle had hoped, having spent two years as a non-league player, he began to explore the possibilities. Non-league was a great place to learn the trade.

It was easy for ex-professionals to go into retirement but for Castle, that wasn't an option. He joined Cambridge United as an assistant as he looked to pursue a coaching career.

'Cambridge was a year as an assistant manager to Jimmy Quinn. It was a professional setup at the time, which it still is [with the club playing in League One]. At the time, they were in the National League and the club were going through hard times, but it was still a privilege to be at the club,' Castle enthused as he looked back on his time at United. 'The club wasn't a shadow of what is it now. It was hard work, but the players were very good. They didn't start very well and the whole season was about trying to keep themselves in the league rather than getting relegated.'

While Cambridge had struggled at the time, it was difficult to see them being in that situation again. The U's had had a turbulent time in the Football League between 1970 and 1990, going up and down between the Football League and Conference, but from 1990 they had their most successful season under manager John Beck. Despite a successful reign for Beck over a three-year period, the club were relegated from the new First Division in 1992/93, months after Beck was sacked. The spiral continued and a final relegation came in 2005 when they were relegated from the Conference, but having won promotion back to the Football League in 2014 they have remained there ever since. The idea of clubs as old as Cambridge being out of the Football League was something people didn't want to get used to. Bolton Wanderers had spent 132 years of their 146-

year existence in the Football League, while Notts County had spent 131 years of their 158 years in the competition before their relegation to the National League in 2019. There were also clubs at the other end of the spectrum who you wouldn't have expected to see in the Football League. Harrogate Town were 106 years old when they reached League Two for the first time in 2020.

The year at Cambridge had only been the start and soon after it had ended, Castle made a swift return to St Albans City. With his time there as a player, the chairman felt it was best for Castle to return to St Albans in a managerial capacity. Although many non-league players and managers had stayed connected with their previous clubs, Castle already had a strong link with St Albans outside of his playing career.

'I always had a link with the club from when I was first there. I had set up a college link – which I am still doing now. The chairman at the time, myself and his wife set that going and thankfully, it is still going today [17 years later]. It has come away from St Albans Football Club and is now part of Oaklands College.'

When Castle returned to St Albans during the 2007/08 season, they weren't in the best position and he was given the job of lifting the team in the league table as well as the club's spirit. St Albans had had three different managers over two seasons before Castle was appointed. Colin Lippiatt was at the helm during 2006/07 but following relegation to Conference South, he was replaced by Ritchie Hanlon. Hanlon was inexperienced and in October 2007 he was replaced by Dave Anderson, who lasted for just short of four months before he became another managerial casualty.

'They weren't going through the best of times and had gone through a number of managers. The chairman called and asked me to come back – albeit in an interim period – and steady the ship, which I did, and the spell lasted longer than I thought,' Castle said.

Castle's time at St Albans had prepared him for any future ventures. After three years at St Albans and a short time coaching, he joined Royston Town as their manager in 2013.

'I was doing taxi driving at the time. On top of being a football coach and driving a taxi, I was also manager of local Step 5 side, Takeley. I was enjoying it, not a problem, but I knew the manager of Royston at the time, and he had done a fantastic job at the club. Unfortunately, he wanted to pull away – he was also a taxi driver and we got talking. He suggested that I went for it, and I was probably ready to come away from Step 5 [Royston were Step 4]. I had heard what a good club it was and went up and spoke via an interview with the board. I was quite fortunate both parties liked each other, and we've carried on since 2013 until now.

'We've been highly successful since I've taken over. We have always been in the top half and never struggled. We had a promotion, whilst accumulating 102 points in the Southern League Division One Central to get into the Premier Division, so that saw us make a step up in the pyramid.'

During the season in which Royston lifted the Division One Central title, Castle had been confident that the Crows would lift the championship. While some leagues offered multiple promotion places each season, it was often the case that only one team would go up, meaning every season would be even more competitive. Clubs would often throw resources at a title push, but it never guaranteed results. The Crows had finished seventh in the Southern League Division One Central in 2013/14, and ten points outside of the play-offs, before finishing in second place the following season. Kettering Town had won the title by 11 points but Castle wanted to take his team closer, finishing second again in 2015/16 but four points behind Kings Langley.

'We were expected to win it every single season. We went about it and got to runners-up two years in a row before that, so we were also going in there with a favourites label, but at the same time, there were always half-decent teams with decent stature like Farnborough who, that year, were spending quite a large budget. It was never going to be easy. We needed to try and take the mantle and win the title outright, otherwise, other than through the play-offs, there were no second chances as it were,' Castle continued as he described the run towards winning the league. 'Halfway through the season it was quite close. Farnborough were doing their best to hang in there, but we beat them 5-0 at home, which gave us a boost and I think it killed them off. I think we went on and won the title by 12 points.'

After their promotion, Royston's first two seasons in the Premier Division saw them finish seventh in 2017/18 and tenth in 2018/19. The following season was a better year for them, both in the league and in the FA Trophy.

Castle said, 'This season [2019/20], we got into the last eight of the FA Trophy, beating well-known teams like Boreham Wood, Chester, Ebbsfleet and Wealdstone. That really helped to make a name for ourselves as a football club. Our aim as a club is to make Royston a recognised team in non-league and with many players wanting to come down and play for the club, I get an awful lot of satisfaction from that.'

Royston found themselves third in 2019/20 and, while the Southern League Premier Division Central season wouldn't be completed, they had a real chance of winning the title and achieving promotion. It also felt like more than just any promotion with a place in National League North or South up for grabs.

'Personally, I thought we were going to go and win it. When you look at it, there were four teams involved. Ourselves and Tamworth were probably in the hot seat. They sat two points above us, having played the same number of games. Peterborough Sports were also two points ahead of us, but had played three games more, so that left us with three games in hand,' said Castle.

'Bromsgrove Sports were also contenders with the number of points they had, but had played two games more. When you look at the run-ins, Tamworth had the tougher run-in to ours. I believe with us having got through to the fourth qualifying round of the [FA] Cup and the last eight of the [FA] Trophy, the lads were buzzing for success off the back of that and I think we would have achieved it, had we been allowed to.'

There was no doubt that Castle had ambitions for Royston. He wanted them to reach higher levels of the pyramid and had confidence they'd reach the National League.

'We've progressed since 2013 from a Step 4 football club into a comfortable Step 3 side. Over the last few years, we've become very competitive at this level, and I would say we would be labelled now as that club. We're swapping blows with recognised football clubs at our level. Nuneaton Borough, who have been in the National [League], Tamworth, who have also been in the National League alongside Stourbridge and Rushden & Diamonds. These are teams that are well known throughout Steps 1 to 3 and we're trading blows with these and even coming out winners.'

Both parties certainly had ambitions to reach the next level. For Royston, it was about reaching the next level in the National League System and, while they were close during 2019/20, once the new season started, their target would remain the same.

Castle said, 'When the time is right, we know that we would be good enough for the National League North or South, although the National League [Step 1] would be a step too far at this moment in time. We're slowly but surely getting a fanbase that we are proud of and it's getting better and better. It's only a little town but growing and the interest that is coming from the community is unheard of. We need to make sure our club is recognised and being thought of by the locals.'

And what of Castle's own personal ambitions?

'There are mates of mine that have managed at Premier League. Wayne Burnett is at Tottenham Hotspur [under-23s] – we were at Orient and Plymouth together. Chris Wilder [who was at Sheffield United] and Eddie Howe [who was at Bournemouth], who I played against several times, have done incredibly well. I wouldn't say at 54 that I am going anywhere near that level but certainly would like to go to a league level and give it a go. I'm realistic enough to know that you get a couple of chances, if you're lucky, and one opportunity. You only have to look at the Cowley Brothers at Portsmouth and see how they progressed through from non-league to a decent League One side. I'm also realistic enough to know there is as good a manager in non-league as there is higher up the pyramid. You have to be so much more of a manager and have to deal with a lot more in non-league than you do at the higher levels. I'm privileged to have had 20-odd years as a player and ten or so in non-league so I think I am quite experienced to make comparisons.'

* * *

Gary Cohen was born into a sporting family, making it highly likely he'd be an athlete too. His mother, Eleanor Thomas, and his father, Glen Cohen, represented Great Britain at athletics, while his aunt, Shirley Thomas, also ran for Team GB. His father had famously won a gold medal at the 1974 Rome European Championships in the 4x100m relay, and his auntie had won two silvers – one at the 1982 Athens European Championships and another at the 1983 Helsinki World Championships, also in the 4x100m relay but for Gary, football was the sport he had chosen.

His parents had held him back from joining an athletics club, but like every young kid, he had played football from a young age and when it came to a choice of running or playing football, he had been too far into football to turn his back on the sport. It was a decision that led him on to big things.

'I was brought up around athletic tracks and it was the sport I would watch most on the telly,' Cohen explained. 'My passion growing up was athletics as I wanted to be like my parents. I remember when I was at Spurs as a kid, the coach asked everyone that wanted to be a footballer to put their hand up. I didn't and told him I wanted to be an athlete but because my parents didn't want me to join an athletics club until I was older and when it came to choosing, I was too involved with football.'

As a young player, he signed for Watford as a trainee. The move hadn't worked out as he had hoped and before he had the chance to sign on a full-time basis, the Hornets wanted to see if he could handle football as a full-time trainee. It had proven to be a tough time for Cohen, who suffered an injury and didn't have the chance to prove himself.

'I didn't actually sign as a full-time trainee as they were unsure whether I could handle full-time football, so the plan was that I would train with the youth teams on the Easter holiday to see how I would cope. Unfortunately, I suffered a hairline fracture in my ankle, so I never got the opportunity to prove that I would be okay. Instead, I trained with the under-16s on a Tuesday and Thursday, then playing with the under-17s on a Saturday.'

Cohen's time at Watford meant he hadn't got close to the first team, but he still got the chance to pull on the yellow shirt for the reserves. For a young player who had dreamt of playing for a professional side, it was a huge hit. He didn't want to see it as a missed opportunity to play for the First Division side as he continued to try and enjoy his football, but he only lasted a season at Vicarage Road as Watford were affected financially by the ITV Digital collapse in 2002. The Hornets were threatened by administration as their financial frailties came to the surface. An agreed 12 per cent pay cut for the players and an FA Cup run brought in much-needed revenue, preventing the club from going down the dark road of administration, but for Cohen, it wasn't enough to keep him at Vicarage Road. He knew he wasn't going to get a contract and he was released at the end of the season.

'I never got close to the first team but played quite a few games for the reserves. This was around the time of the ITV Digital collapse and the clubs affected were cutting costs where they could. I knew I hadn't done enough to warrant a contract extension so that wasn't a surprise to be told that. I don't think I really thought of it as a release, possibly because I knew it was coming.'

It hadn't taken Cohen long to find a new club as he signed for non-league Scarborough, linking up with Russell Slade. Slade had joined the Seadogs in 2001 when they looked doomed at the bottom of the Conference, but he had managed to save them. This was Cohen's first experience of non-league football. Non-league was tough for young players who had little experience of senior football, but he fought through and enjoyed playing against experienced players. Young footballers who had only played in academies were not as well off when it came to senior appearances, so non-league taught them how to be tough and it was no different for Cohen.

'Growing up, I got to know the Holdsworth twins well and David [Holdsworth] was at Scarborough at the time. One of my old coaches put me back in touch with him and he spoke to the manager. I was invited down for a trial game against Mansfield, and I stood out with my pace and fearlessness, so they signed me until the end of the season.

'I loved it. I was playing against men and seasoned players. A lot of the players were old pros and knew every trick in the book. Academy football is great and allows players to build their foundations as a footballer, but nothing comes close to non-league as it takes you out of your comfort zone. While you still had your technical players, a lot of the games felt rugged and almost felt like a survival of the fittest sport as the tempo was a lot quicker than academy football.'

Cohen spent a season in the Conference, but in 2004/05, although he had begun preparations with Scarborough, his career had taken its next move. Cohen wasn't happy with what he had been offered at the Conference side so travelled over the border to Scotland and was back in a professional setup, albeit a very different one to what he had experienced at Watford. While he was a youth player at the Hornets, the move to Gretna was his first professional side as a senior player, giving it a completely different feel altogether.

'I had started pre-season with Scarborough, but a couple of things had left a sour taste in my mouth. One of them was that they offered me a one-year full-time deal but gave me a contract for 38 weeks. I never used an agent, so it felt like they were trying their luck.

'David Holdsworth had signed for Scottish side Gretna and asked me to go with him. Initially, I had said no but after incident number two, I decided to follow David up there. Even then, I was a firm believer that if you're happy, you play well. The owner of Gretna happened to think the same way as me which was great.'

Gretna had been elected to the Scottish Football League two years before he put pen to paper, making a tremendous rise up the divisions. In Cohen's time at the club they won the Division Three, Division Two and Division One titles in successive seasons between 2005 and 2007, but for Cohen it hadn't quite worked out. In his first season he had failed to hit the heights that people had expected and as a result he found himself loaned out to non-league Workington AFC.

A move that seemed perfect for Cohen had seen him return to the lower levels with Workington, in the Northern Premier League Premier Division (Step 3), but he didn't let that bother him and he sought to make the loan move pay off with a return to Gretna on the horizon that season.

'My first season at Gretna was not as expected and I didn't live up to expectation. I found myself out of the squad, I got sent off when coming off the bench and dragged at half-time in another game. When the season ended, I went away and re-evaluated before getting myself fit for the start of pre-season. It was a change to what the first season was as I was flying and enjoying myself. The first-team manager had been away for the first two weeks, but the assistant manager was buzzing with me and telling me the manager would be excited to see me like this,' Cohen explained.

When the manager did return, it was a different story to what Cohen had expected. He was called into the office and told he should go out on loan before the manager had even seen him training, another hit to what Cohen felt would have been a better time in his career. The desire of the manager was to send him out to a Scottish non-league club but that wasn't an option.

'I had already experienced racist remarks in the league, and I wasn't prepared to potentially open myself up to more in the Scottish non-league pyramid. Fortunately, Workington knew about me and wanted me to sign. I told the manager, and his comments were, "If you do well, you can stay there for the season." In my head I thought, surely if I do well, you want me back.'

Playing back in England had done Cohen wonders as he got back to enjoying his football. Workington were also flying in the league as they sought to win the first

Northern Premier League play-offs. After the 2003/04 season, the top 14 sides had been placed in the Premier Division from the First Division (Step 4) as the league was restructured, meaning Workington were one of those to go up. They had finished seventh during that season but after 42 games in 2004/05 they were second, qualifying for the play-offs. Hyde United had finished top of the league with 88 points and were three points ahead of the Reds, winning their second consecutive, title having been First Division champions the previous season.

The play-offs were contested by Workington, Farsley Celtic, Whitby Town and Prescot Cables, with Burscough missing out by a single point. The semi-finals took place on 14 May 2005, with Farsley at home to Whitby and Workington at home to Prescot. Farsley beat Whitby 1-0 after extra time while the Reds were 3-1 winners over Prescot.

The final itself was another tight battle between the two sides. After 90 minutes and a period of extra time, the match remained goalless and was settled from the spot. To the delight of Cohen and his team-mates, it was Workington who were promoted after winning 6-5 on penalties, sending them up to Conference North (Step 2).

'We, as a team, were flying, and I found my own individual form. I was playing with a smile on my face and loved every minute of it. That football suited me a lot better for whatever reason, maybe the game was played at a faster pace than Scotland. We ended up winning the play-offs and got promoted into the Conference North. If I remember rightly, there was a team that got kicked out of the league and there was a furore about the league positions, so the play-offs were delayed.'

Spennymoor United had resigned from the Northern Premier League after 33 league games due to the misfortune of the club folding, and the controversy of how their remaining fixtures would be dealt with rocked the league. Initially, the NPL decided to expunge the results of Spennymoor, but Workington – alongside Gateshead, Radcliffe Borough and Hyde – appealed to the Football Association to get the decision overturned and the FA recommended that the NPL withdraw their decision to void Spennymoor's results. Despite the advice, the league confirmed it would expunge the results a day after the final day of the season, but the standings were different to how they had eventually finished. Cohen's Workington had finished top with Hyde in second and Farsley third, but Hyde had played a game fewer due to their fixture with Spennymoor not going ahead. Another appeal from the same four clubs led to the FA overturning the NPL's decision, making it clear they would not be expelled, nor their results expunged. This meant the remaining sides who didn't play their games against Spennymoor were awarded three points, but neither the goals for nor against were affected by the decision.

The table changed overnight and Workington, who had found themselves top after the final day of the season, having played a game more, were overtaken by Hyde after they were one of the sides awarded points. Burscough were also affected. They had finished fifth and in the play-offs, but with six points given to Prescot, due to having two games against Spennymoor that didn't get played during the season, the sides swapped positions with the point difference. Despite attempts to appeal the decision from Farsley and Burscough, Hyde were presented with the championship trophy and the delayed play-offs went ahead.

With a smile back on his face after a fantastic season with Workington, Cohen's loan spell had come to an end, and he made his way back to Scotland and back to Gretna. He made his way back into the manager's office to discuss his future. He was excited for what could be on the cards but after he stepped into the office, his mood changed.

'I walked in there and said, "Before you say anything, I know you don't want me, so I'll find another club to go on loan to." He said I had taken the words out of his mouth. I had protected myself from more heartache as I always had an inkling when bad news was on its way.'

As he searched for another club with his future on his mind, Cohen had another chat with David Holdsworth. David had got back in touch with Russell Slade, who had moved to Grimsby Town in 2004. Slade had always been a safe bet for Cohen, having previously played for him, so any approval of a move was good enough for him. With the manager's blessing, he made a loan move to League Two Grimsby for the 2005/06 season.

'For me, any chance to play in the EFL, even if it were just substitute appearances, would be something I could build on. Russell was keen and I signed on loan for a season.

I don't think either of us expected me to become a first-team regular but that's what happened, making the right-hand side of midfield my own. I think we, as a team, really surprised everyone. We had a good cup run and were league [title] contenders for most of the season.'

The season had got off to a decent start for Grimsby as they were defeated just twice in the opening six games. A draw on the opening day with Oxford United was followed by their first victory just three days later as they beat Bristol Rovers away from home. Their brief unbeaten start was ended with a narrow 1-0 loss to Darlington at home before wins against Barnet and Rushden & Diamonds got them back to winning ways, but their second defeat, 3-1 to Stockport County, started September in the worst possible way. Wins against Chester City, Peterborough United and Torquay United then came in the space of 11 days before draws against Boston United and Shrewsbury Town either side of a 4-0 victory against Notts County added to that run – Cohen had also scored his first League Two goal for Grimsby in the victory over County. The run was ended with a narrow loss to Wycombe Wanderers before the Mariners struggled to find the same form again, but 15 wins between late November and the end of the season in May were enough to boost Grimsby to the play-offs, ending up fourth behind Leyton Orient, who had finished three points above Town to nab the final automatic promotion place. The season had looked set to finish on a high, with Town finding themselves top of the league and having spent large parts of the season in the automatic places, but Carlisle United, Northampton Town and Orient had surpassed them, meaning they had to settle for the route of the play-offs.

Cohen had contributed a further five goals throughout the season – two of the most important coming against Bury in a 2-1 win and against Oxford United in a 3-2 victory. It was no secret that Cohen enjoyed playing in the Football League, even if he did like what non-league offered. With the season going well and Grimsby making the play-offs, the number of supporters in League Two was certainly a boost for the players as they sought to achieve promotion to League One.

'As much as I love the intimacy of non-league football and how you get to know the fans really well, for me, you can't beat playing in front of a large crowd,' Cohen said. 'When we were doing well, I think we would have 3,000 to 4,000 attending our games. The games against Tottenham Hotspur and Newcastle United [in the League Cup] were around 8,000. The fans truly gave us a buzz when they got behind us and that certainly lifted our game. It was actually surreal.'

Grimsby had been joined by Cheltenham Town, Wycombe Wanderers and Lincoln City in the play-offs, with the Mariners up against Lincoln. In the other semi-final, Cheltenham beat Wycombe 2-1 over the two legs to put them into the final. A Gary Jones goal was enough for a 1-0 victory in the first leg for Grimsby before, three days later, another Jones goal and one from Ben Futcher set up a final with the Robins. It was played at the Millennium

Stadium, Cardiff, but despite the enthusiasm, it wasn't to be Grimsby's day as they were defeated 1-0. The loss was a difficult one to take and it was made even more tough given where they had found themselves throughout the season. The play-offs had offered Grimsby a second chance to achieve promotion but they had fallen short in the final.

'The play-off loss was tough to take. We had been automatic promotion contenders all season and stuttered at the end. We had our rivals [Lincoln] in the semi-finals before we couldn't find enough in the final despite doing all the hard work. Even though I knew it was coming, I was still disappointed to be on the bench, but my form hadn't warranted a start. That game [against Cheltenham], we were flat in our performance, and they narrowly beat us. Even to this day, I can't put my finger on why we were flat, but I think it's worse knowing that, if we had performed anywhere close to our best, we would have been promoted.'

Midway through the 2005/06 season Cohen had joined Grimsby on a permanent transfer from Gretna, but the following campaign became one to forget. A pre-season injury saw him continually break down at regular intervals and without a sight of his condition improving, he departed Grimsby, who finished 15th, 12 points outside of the play-offs.

'My season didn't materialise at all,' Cohen explained. 'I got injured during pre-season and had knee surgery before spending the season breaking down in training. It was so frustrating. The club and I reached an agreement to terminate my contract because of the constant relapses.'

Cohen was out of football for two years due to injury, including his final season at Grimsby, but once he had recovered he was looking to get back into football and turned to non-league. He joined St Albans City ahead of the 2008/09 season, linking up with another manager he knew in Steve Castle.

'I was missing it and my knee felt good. Steve was the manager of St Albans City. I had known him for most of my life so decided to link up with him. I went training with them, but the first session was tough. I felt so rusty and out of my depth, but the more sessions I took part in, the better I felt. The most important thing was that my knee wasn't giving me any trouble whatsoever.'

Cohen spent two seasons at St Albans, 2008/09 and 2009/10, making 81 league appearances and scoring 12 goals. In that first season, St Albans finished 12th in Conference South. Castle had given the team a target of promotion, but after a poor run of form they slipped down to their final league position. The following season had been no better as they finished 13th, although they had collected more points than in 2008/09. It was tough for City as they battled against the likes of Newport County, Dover Athletic and AFC Wimbledon over the course of two seasons but, with little success under Castle, Cohen left St Albans at the end of 2009/10.

In 2010 he stopped playing completely. While Cohen was playing non-league football he had also been working, as the lower levels paid very little, if anything, and certainly not enough to live off. As he searched for a better job, he answered an advertisement to join the ambulance service but the rota he was on meant football wasn't an option.

Cohen said, 'After my professional football career had come to an end, I was bouncing between jobs that didn't pay particularly well or offer great long-term stability. The trouble I found was that no one was willing to give me a chance because my background was football. I decided to give the ambulance service a go after seeing a job advert, but I was working seven out of ten weekends, so football wasn't sustainable. It was gutting having to stop playing, but finding a job was a real struggle and once I had weighed up the option, joining the ambulance service made more sense.'

Cohen's time in the ambulance service had seen him spend five years away from football but he felt he needed to make a return. The fire had still been burning inside and he laced up his boots once again, returning to non-league football in 2015 and linking up with Castle once again as he signed for Royston Town. Castle had played a big part in Cohen's return to the lower levels and when he was asked to play for his old boss again, he put pen to paper and pulled on the white shirt of the Crows.

'I loved it [playing for Royston]. There were so many elements to it that I missed; forgetting my worries for 90 minutes, competing to better your opponent, feeling the benefits of physical exercise, being part of a team, the atmosphere that was generated in a changing room and the feeling of winning.'

Cohen spent just over two years at Royston, winning promotion in 2016/17. His first season with the club had seen them finish second before they marched to the title after winning 32 of their 42 games. He had gone into a third season with Royston but made the move across Step 4 of the National League System with a switch to AFC Hornchurch of Isthmian League North Division. The transfer came about as he wanted to continue playing but found himself out of the manager's plans, although he didn't want that to affect him.

'I joined Hornchurch after leaving Royston. I wasn't in the gaffer's plan as much as I wanted to be so decided to move on. Jimmy Mac [McFarlane] was the manager at the time, and I happened to bump into his son in Romford. Before I knew it, I was signing for them, but I didn't mention this to Royston at the time. The feeling [at the club] was the same. It felt like a family, which I had at the majority of non-league clubs I had played for. I hadn't experienced that at professional clubs, but I think that was down to the size of these clubs and the amount of people involved. I loved my time at Hornchurch, and it was a shame I wasn't part of the title-winning side.'

Cohen's time with the Urchins had come to an end and during the 2017/18 season, he made the switch across the North Division to Soham Town Rangers. Hornchurch were the eventual winners of the division after racking up 103 points, beating Potters Bar to the title by 13 points, while Bowers & Pitsea, Haringey Borough and Heybridge Swifts weren't far behind the runners-up. Soham, on the other hand, had finished 13th with 58 points but had still finished above top sides in Grays Athletic, Waltham Abbey and Brentwood Town.

'I had played with Mass [Rob Mason] and Erks [Erkan Okay] at Royston Town and they asked me to come down. They did a fantastic job that season and are continuing to do so. If they were closer, I probably wouldn't have left when I did,' said Cohen.

The travelling had been a slight issue, so he preferred playing for a team that was closer. His next move was to Barking after manager Justin Gardener had asked him to go over to the Blues. Although he had started at the Blues, by Christmas, he was no longer a non-league player because of changing off-field circumstances.

'I then joined Barking after Justin contacted me on Twitter and we had a good conversation. Unfortunately, after Christmas, I had to hang up my boots up again because I was working full-time, about to start a diploma and had a young family. It was a difficult decision to step away from football again, but my circumstances didn't allow for the freedom of football,' said Cohen.

4

Up for the Cup

WHEN THE football season begins in August – sometimes as early as the end of July – so do the earlier rounds of the FA Cup. Some 368 clubs are entered into the extra preliminary round, with a further 276 joining throughout the qualifying rounds as they try to battle their way to the dreamland, the first round proper. Although it is months away and requires luck and hard work, it doesn't stop the little local teams dreaming of what could be. Before the so-called big boys get involved, the FA Cup filters through the lower levels.

'There are three things I love about the FA Cup. It was the original football competition, so it connects the origins of football with today. It always involves clubs right down to level ten of the football pyramid, playing across August to May, so it's the only competition that directly connects the Premier League to the lower levels and every game has intensity, suspense, interest and meaning. It's a knockout competition. One defeat and you're out. There are no second chances,' said Phil Annets, the creator of the FA Cup Factfile database and website.

Annets created the Factfile in 2015, updating it throughout the years, but he had been keeping track of results for as long as he could remember.

'I've always had an interest in football statistics and when I was growing up, the FA Cup Final was the only domestic match shown on TV, so it had a strong fascination to me. As a consequence, I collated as much information about the competition as possible. So, you could argue that I've been working on the FA Cup Factfile all my life, updating it season after season, but I only launched my research publicly in 2015.

'I knew I had a comprehensive database of the FA Cup teams and matches, but I also knew it could have always been improved upon. I put it out into the footballing world in the hope to make it as accurate as possible. On top of that, I was quite often correcting the mistakes in other people's tweets and blogs on the FA Cup. In particular, I noticed there was little being produced about the non-league clubs in the competition. The FA Cup Factfile covers all 3,500-plus clubs who have ever participated in the FA Cup over its near 150-year existence.

'It's critical to publicise the involvement of non-league clubs in the FA Cup and to make everyone aware that the competition isn't just for the top sides. The passion for the FA Cup from those involved with clubs which start in August is immense. I wish that the owners and managers of Premier League clubs could attend these early qualifying round matches and talk with those club owners, fans, volunteers, board members, players and coaching staff to see the passion that exists amongst them for the competition first hand.

'Maybe they would treat the FA Cup with more respect and not use it as a try-out for younger or fringe players.

'For many non-league clubs, the prize money earned on a good FA Cup run could be the difference between existence and going out of business. Yes, the potential money is fantastic and could keep a club going for seasons to come, but it is only a potential. What the fans, players, board members, coaches and volunteers really love about being involved in the FA Cup is the connectivity with the most well-known Football League and Premier League clubs. It's about the chance to make memories. To be able to say that you've participated in the same competition as the likes of Harry Kane, Mohamed Salah and Sergio Agüero is something that will stick with them forever. Especially if you scored a goal in the competition, or even get to face some professional players.'

Flicking through his database of results, Annets had plenty to choose from, but it was clear what club run he enjoyed the most. Above being the creator of the Factfile, Annets was still the supporter of a Premier League side. Despite supporting Leeds, however, he couldn't help but enjoy watching lower-league teams in the competition.

'From a club supporter's point of view, it has to be Leeds United's cup win in 1972. Saying that, I remember more through repeat viewings than I do from what I recollected at the time.

'Since I launched the Factfile, I have visited many football clubs around the country. Most of them are local village sides. One of my favourite moments was when I visited Hook Norton for their biggest ever FA Cup game against Weston-super-Mare during the 2015/16 season. I was in the bar looking for a team sheet when I spotted an elderly gent who seemed to be part of the club. I asked him if there were any team sheets available, and instead of handing me a printed version, he held up a small whiteboard with players listed on it. I photographed him holding the whiteboard, thanked him for his help and asked what his role at the club was. He told me he was the chairman – brilliant! Imagine having that experience at a Premier League club.'

The format of the competition guarantees that several non-league clubs will reach the dreamland of the first round proper when League One and Two sides are entered into the fray. While the league sides hope for a draw against the part-timers, thinking it would be a walkover into the next round, the non-league clubs hope for the biggest opposition at the time, usually top of the league in League One. With over 600 non-league teams going through the qualifying rounds, fewer than five per cent will make it to the first round proper.

'Thirty-two non-league clubs qualify for the FA Cup first round proper each season, but it's really important the media highlights these clubs' achievement. Seeing non-league clubs pitting their skills against Football League sides is, to a lot of people, what the FA Cup is all about,' said Annets.

The coverage of the earlier rounds has always been rare, although the BBC did manage to choose a game to host on their website while BT Sport would try to send journalists around the grounds, reporting on the action. It was hard to see this as a positive. For clubs in the lower leagues it was great to feature on TV, but many of the reporters didn't know the level of football while it was difficult to find the results anywhere other than club Twitter accounts. The BBC would have pages of fixtures from each round, but didn't always update them as they would for more well-known clubs. Instead, they would be updated hours or even days later.

'The mainstream media need to do more to shine a light on these clubs, especially their exploits from August onwards. When the FA Cup is being reviewed with progress to date, it starts at the first round and ignores all that has gone before it,' said Annets.

In recent seasons the BBC has tried to show at least one live game from each round, starting from the extra preliminary round. Clubs drawn against bigger opposition were gifted the opportunity to feature on the television, while the BBC also tried to show footage captured by the fans in goal compilations. The coverage, however, didn't match the prize money given to those clubs. Ahead of the 2020/21 season, the prize money throughout the competition was halved. That didn't really affect the eventual winners as they still received £1.8m, but for the clubs starting in the extra preliminary round, that meant £2,250 becoming £1,125, and the first qualifying round (two rounds later) going from £4,500 to £2,250. Just from the extra preliminary and preliminary rounds alone, non-league clubs missed out on a combined £584,000, but the loser of the semi-final still received £450,000. The clubs who reached the first round proper and beyond would receive TV money, at least 45 per cent of gate receipts for each game they were involved in and a payment from a pooled percentage of all gate receipts.

League Two Leyton Orient were stunned during the 2019/20 season in the first round proper when they were beaten by Maldon & Tiptree. The Isthmian League North Division side had progressed through five qualifying rounds before being rewarded with a trip to east London. While it doesn't happen often, there are always rare glimpses of magic when it comes to the FA Cup.

'Everyone remembers the giantkillings of old. The BBC never tire to show us the Hereford United defeat of Newcastle United whenever the FA Cup third round comes around. In this day and age, it's becoming increasingly difficult for non-league clubs to beat top-flight sides. Lincoln City was an exception and did just that during the 2016/17 season, winning [1-0] at Burnley,' said Annets.

'Even when there are non-league clubs in the competition by the third round and beyond, the TV companies often ignore them to show an all-Premier League clash instead. I believe that if a club has fought through at least three rounds of the FA Cup to reach the third round, they should automatically be selected as a live match. It would reinforce the broad nature of the competition and how it is for everyone.'

* * *

Chichester City wrote themselves into FA Cup history during the 2019/20 season. Having begun their journey at the very first stage, the extra preliminary round, they battled their way to the second round proper. It was clear that the FA Cup was the priority for the club.

'If you've seen our history, the club many years ago did something very similar,' said coach Daniel Potter. 'As a management team, we have been at the club for the last five years, but we haven't been able to get beyond the preliminary round for the last three seasons. When we went into the cup this season, we had the expectation of getting through the preliminary rounds and seeing how far we could get. We had no expectation we would get as far as we did.

'This was our first season as a Step 4 side, having been promoted the season before. We strengthened the squad for what was needed to compete in a new league, and we prepared ourselves to prioritise the FA Cup and the league as the two competitions we wanted to focus on. Other cup competitions like the county cup and the FA Trophy weren't our focus and we took our eyes away from those. As a result, we suffered quite heavily in those competitions by being knocked out early. We have since reflected on that decision, but we still feel it was the right thing to do.'

Chichester had been playing in the Southern Combination League Premier Division, winning the 2018/19 title by nine points ahead of Horsham YMCA. The promotion from Step 5 to Step 4 meant the club would not feature in the FA Vase, instead taking part in the FA Trophy, but it didn't change where they started in the FA Cup. With the club aiming to get through the preliminary round, they achieved what they wanted. Having beaten Erith Town in the extra preliminary round they were then drawn away to Bridon Ropes.

'When you look at the teams and realise you are playing a step or two below, you know you have a good chance, but you have to be wary of the underdog who will always want to battle and work hard,' said Potter.

Braces for Scott Jones, Kaleem Haitham and Gicu Lordache, and a goal for Callum Overton, helped City to an incredible 7-2 win over Bridon. Chichester would have been expected to beat their opponents, who sat two levels below them, but they still needed to get the job done.

Potter said, 'I recall the day very well. It was a very hot day. We got there early and prepared ourselves for the test ahead. The message to the players was no different to what it would be in a league game; we needed to do whatever it took to get a win. When our players adapt themselves well against lower opposition, we tend to dominate and control games from the start and that's what we did against Bridon Ropes.'

While they had fought through the initial stages, the qualifying rounds would only get harder. Non-league clubs had to fight through four qualifying rounds after getting through the preliminary round and that was just to reach the first round proper. After beating Chalfont St Peter 2-0 in the first qualifying round, Chichester were drawn against Hartley Wintney. It was by far the toughest game they had faced during the 2019/20 season. City certainly weren't favourites as they came up against their first Step 3 side.

'We knew a little about Hartley in the preparations for the game. That again was a hot day. The pitch was hard, and the conditions weren't ideal. We knew as the game was growing old, we were lucky to have stayed in the tie and it was clear they were the better team on the occasion, but the draw was a good result for us. When we got to the latter stages of the game, we were holding on, knowing we could take them to a replay,' said Potter.

That game finished 0-0 and City survived in the competition for another day, bringing Wintney back to Oaklands Park for a replay. It was often the case that lower-league sides would be happy to get a replay at their home ground, giving them a better chance of progression. The hosts had come close to the first round proper in the recent years but fell short several times. Like Chichester, they wanted to reach the holy grail, but it was City who used that to their advantage.

'The replay was a different game. It was on our pitch, which was much better, and the weather was kinder. It was an evening game, so it was nowhere near as hot. We adapted much better as a team to the playing surface and deserved the win,' said Potter, recalling the 1-0 win in the replay. 'We played with more character, and we looked after the ball a lot better when playing at home.'

The victory meant that Chichester had fought their way through four rounds and were only two wins away from being one of the non-league sides in the first round proper. Despite being so close, they didn't want to get carried away and think too far ahead. It would have been hard to regain focus if they got distracted by the prospect of reaching the dreamland.

'The only time we really looked forward to the proper rounds was when we reached the fourth qualifying round. When we played Hartley Wintney, Enfield Town and even earlier than that, when we played clubs like Chalfont St Peter, we were looking at each game in isolation. It was only against Bowers & Pitsea that we looked at the possibility of reaching the first round. Had we thought that earlier on, it probably wouldn't have happened.'

As they got deeper into the competition, the ties got tougher for Chichester and once the Isthmian League Premier Division sides entered the draw, City welcomed one of the most well-known teams to Oaklands Park. Enfield were the visitors in the third qualifying round, but that didn't faze the squad.

'The Enfield game was tough. We were lucky to get the draw at home. We felt fortunate that went our way because we were going up against a very good Isthmian League side. We knew a little bit about them, and in our eyes, we played them at a very good time,' said Potter.

The underdog always felt more confident playing at home. Having a bigger support and playing on a surface they were used to, always helped. Playing at home didn't guarantee a positive result but it gave the City more belief. Although it looked like a tough game, Potter felt there was no better time to welcome the Towners to the club.

Potter revealed, 'They had their centre-back unavailable, and in the previous week, they lost another very good attacking player to suspension. Without two of their better players, we knew that was our chance. The game was very tight, and we managed to nick it, 1-0. We got our goal late on, but we gave ourselves a very good opportunity to beat them that day. The way we prepared ourselves with detail, set pieces and having gone to see them play, we gave ourselves the opportunity to beat them and we did.'

The win had started to make people notice Chichester as a giantkiller. Although the earlier rounds had seen them beat teams from the level below, they had also progressed past Step 4 opposition before taking on two Step 3 sides and winning. Having narrowly beaten Enfield, Chichester drew another Isthmian League Premier Division side, Bowers & Pitsea, out of the hat. They were now only one game from reaching the proper rounds of the FA Cup but couldn't lose focus on the task in hand.

'The Bowers game was difficult because we had started to make more noise ourselves. Many people were taking an interest at that stage as to how well we were doing and how far we had come. The gap between us and Bowers was a lot closer than that of Enfield. They didn't have the greatest league form and, for us, we looked at them as not being much greater than us performance-wise. We believed we were one of the better teams in the league,' said Potter.

The confidence shown by the management and players had paid off as Chichester managed to beat Bowers & Pitsea away from home. Defender Max Axell gave City the lead in the 16th minute before Kaleem Haitham doubled the advantage just seven minutes later. A resilient effort from Chichester saw them block out Bowers' advances until the 90th minute when Max Cornhill pulled one back for the home side. It was another narrow win but certainly one of the biggest in the club's history as they had navigated their way to the first round proper. It had been a simple case of Chichester understanding their opponents and stepping up on the day.

'The biggest thing about the game was whoever won on the day, was going to be breaking a club record [for how far they got]. Both sides wanted to be there, but we were fortunate in the way we started the game. We got two early goals. One was quite lucky, but we also got a penalty. Some may say it was harsh, but I thought it was one [a clear penalty]. As the game grew older, they threw everything at us. We had to try and hold on. When they pulled one back, it was quite tense towards the end, but we felt we had done enough in the end with our preparation and, fortunately, it went our way,' Potter explained.

'We were fearful going into the game but the best thing about Bowers was they play on a 4G pitch. We understand how to play on a 4G, but the pitch didn't necessarily benefit either side. We just understood what we needed to do. It was a difficult journey to get there, and we took a lot of fans with us.'

Club officials, players and fans gathered in the clubhouse just two days later as they looked on at the first round draw. The BBC had taken cameras down to Chichester to catch the reaction as the names were pulled out of the hat while the draw was taking place over 100 miles away. All the teams in the draw knew there would be a bye up for grabs as Bury FC were out of the competition. The Bury situation meant they had been expelled from League One and any cup competitions they were due to enter. The bye made it fair for another club not to be unfairly excluded due to the reduced number of teams in the competition, so the Football Association offered passage to the second round proper.

'We knew a lot about it [the bye] when we went in. We had a lot of cameras filming the boys watching the draw live. Originally, the club were shortlisted to host the draw but that was given to Maldon & Tiptree. Our manager and goalkeeper headed down to Maldon to watch the draw and were interviewed beforehand. The hope for us in the first round was to pull a professional team. That is all we wanted,' said Potter.

Once 47 League One and Two teams joined the 32 non-league sides in the draw, Chichester could have come up against anyone. League One leaders Ipswich Town were the highest-ranked side in the competition, but with the club being along the south coast, the majority of Chichester's players favoured a tie against a team closer to home.

Potter looked back, 'The dream was to draw Portsmouth because of the locality and a lot of our players are supporters of the club. That was the dream locally, but as the draw went on, we were very aware of the bye. The assumption was it was never going to be your team. It's hard to think that way but as the teams went down, it was only us and a number of professional teams so the outcome would have been a win-win.'

Chichester were ball number 71. Before the draw, broadcaster Mark Chapman joked that having a single ball left in the pot at the end of the draw usually meant it hadn't been done properly, but this time around it was exactly what would be happening. The players had a particular eye on the ball number 35, Portsmouth, but they would be happy with whoever they drew. Ipswich were out first and had drawn Lincoln City. As the draw went on, so did the potential opponents for Chichester. The dream tie of Pompey had gone within a minute of the draw starting as they were pitted against Harrogate Town of the National League, while the other non-league clubs were also pulled out of the hat. As the draw reached the final five clubs – Chichester, MK Dons, Peterborough United, Port Vale and Stevenage – they still hadn't been pulled out.

The last part of the draw had been made. MK Dons had drawn Port Vale, while Stevenage had been paired with Peterborough, leaving Chichester as the last team in the hat and the recipients of the bye into the second round. The representatives watching the draw down at Maldon hugged and embraced, while the scenes in the clubhouse back in Chichester were of overwhelming joy. Those who had watched on hugged, jumped about and celebrated and they had every reason to.

Potter said, 'When our name famously didn't get pulled out of the hat, that for us was an unbelievable feeling. The club would be more financially secured than it had been in previous years but, more excitingly for the boys, we were in the second round where we had another chance to face a professional side. Just seeing our name in the hat and Chichester being mentioned in the first round draw was a special feeling. Getting to the first round made us feel like we had won the cup and that alone was an amazing achievement for us, so no matter what happened that day, we made history. The cameras caught the moment nicely and we rightly celebrated.

'Anyone who feels we were wrong to celebrate doesn't understand non-league football like we do. It would have been great to play Bury and that would have been the right decision. That wasn't to do with us [why Bury weren't there] and as a football club, we picked up on the opportunity to get into the next round.'

With the prize money they received from progressing, City wanted to help Bury. The town had lost its football club but there were already plans to build a new team to join the National League System towards the lower leagues. Although those plans were still a fair way out, Chichester were still keen to help.

'We understood the financial trouble they were going through, and our chairman was adamant, we would support them in whatever way we could. It was disappointing not to have Bury there but it was well documented as to why they weren't and why there was an extra place for a team to go through. We didn't have any contact with them before that [the draw] but what we did do was reach out to them. The phoenix of Bury, whoever that will be, will need a lot of support and there is a lot that can be done to help in moving forward. It was right to mention that we'd support them,' said Potter

By the time the second-round draw had come around, Chichester were excited at the prospect of who they would face. Almost all of the League One and Two sides had progressed; Portsmouth, Peterborough and Ipswich were still potential options. What made the draw even more special was the choice to hold it at Oaklands Park, City's home ground, with fans, players and management watching on. They had been chosen as they remained as the lowest-ranked side in the competition. They were joined by many other non-league teams who had themselves beaten higher opposition; Maldon & Tiptree had beaten Leyton Orient, Kingstonian had beaten a troubled Macclesfield Town and Altrincham had beaten York City.

Chichester's players had still hoped for the prospect of playing Portsmouth, who were due to play Harrogate on the night of the draw. When their number was pulled out, time stood still as the club watched on, hoping number 40 would be the next number out of the hat. It wasn't and instead, Altrincham were drawn away to Pompey. City didn't have to wait long though as ball number 30, Tranmere Rovers or

Wycombe Wanderers, was pulled out of the hat, followed by 40. A roar of cheers and applause rang around the club as City were guaranteed a League One side. Tranmere then beat Wycombe 2-1 after extra time at Adams Park, meaning the Lilywhites would travel to Prenton Park. It was far from disappointing for the Isthmian League side as they would travel to a team that sat five levels above them in League One.

'The opportunity to play a professional side was huge. We would have preferred playing a team at home but only because we felt we could have had an advantage. There was no doubt, our players were thinking of playing a Premier League team in the third round and some of them were dreaming of playing their boyhood clubs,' said Potter.

Before they could think that far ahead, they had a tie against Tranmere on the horizon. Ahead of the game, the League One side hadn't had the best of form. Of the 17 league games they had played before the FA Cup second round they had only won four, while drawing four and losing nine. They also sat just above the relegation zone in 20th. For Chichester, though, it was a different story. They had only played ten games in the Isthmian League South East Division, winning five and losing just twice. If there was ever a good enough time to play a league team, it was now.

Potter said, 'We knew what a great team Tranmere were and a team with such a rich history. When we realised we were away from home, it was great because the boys had a chance to play at a professional ground in front of a large crowd. For us as a club, it was a great experience to have local and national coverage as well as having it broadcasted on TV.'

The game itself was a step too far as Chichester's run came to an end, losing 5-1. The scoreline didn't reflect how the game had gone but the gap between the sides certainly showed. The game had remained goalless after 60 minutes before a series of goals in quick succession saw Rovers run away with the result. Corey Blackett-Taylor and Morgan Ferrier scored two minutes apart and then another two goals from Ferrier in four minutes gave Tranmere a 4-0 lead. Blackett-Taylor got his brace in the 85th minute, which sealed the victory, but before the match was out the Isthmian League side had their special moment as Ryan Peake scored for the visitors in the first added minute after he headed in a corner from Max Axtell.

'For us, we were proud of what our team achieved [in the competition] but even what happened in that game. We held a professional side for over 60 minutes and one that is five divisions above us. An hour is a really long time in football,' said Potter. 'We knew that physically and psychologically we would start to drain and struggle as we got into the latter stages of the game. They scored four goals quickly before getting their fifth. We played with passion and for us to get a goal at the end was right for the occasion. We celebrated the goal and rightly so!'

Despite the result, Chichester could hold their heads high. They had made the whole of the city proud and had also put the area on the map. While some felt disappointed about the result, the majority were proud. Chichester were never going to win the FA Cup but they had done well enough to get that far.

'Losing the game, we were not disappointed at all. There might have been a little disappointment from one or two of the players [from mistakes they made] but that wouldn't have made a difference. Tranmere were the better side over 90 minutes and, although we believed we were good, we were nowhere near the better team on the day,' said Potter.

'In the first half, we had chances to cause an upset and that meant we could have found ourselves leading 1-0. I felt that we scared them. The goal wouldn't have made much of a difference in the end, and I think they would have won regardless of how we played, but who know how the game would have gone if we were ahead. Very strangely, we celebrated that game.'

Potter looked back at the journey that he and the club had gone on. They navigated their way through six rounds just to be in the first round proper – the same number of wins needed for a Premier League side to lift the trophy.

'It's exciting,' he exclaimed. 'We worked hard and played a lot of games in a condensed period of time. Physically, it was very hard to play the number of games we did, and it put us behind in our league campaign. The idea that we played as many games as the team that's likely to go on to win it is an extraordinary achievement. It shows what a side like Chichester could do and what other non-league sides could achieve. It was, for us, a rollercoaster because we weren't expecting it and we didn't know what was around the corner.'

For many non-league clubs the FA Cup brings in some much-needed financial support, which was definitely the case for City who picked up over £80,000 in prize money.

'The money we picked up was fantastic and it was life-changing for the club. We are going to do things that the club couldn't have dreamt of doing. A couple of years ago, we were in financial trouble and non-league clubs are in that same position,' Potter explained. 'It has given us a safety net to let us know we are going to be all right for the next few seasons.'

The prize money Chichester had picked up during their 2019/20 run would make them stable enough without having another incredible run in the seasons that followed. The rewards for victory really increase in the first round proper but when it comes to the distribution of the prize money, not many clubs reached that far. Potter felt the cash should have been redistributed across the earlier rounds, giving clubs lower down the pyramid a fairer share of the wealth.

'The money is huge for non-league, and I wish the FA addressed it more. I would've liked them to put more money into the earlier rounds of the FA Cup. The team that usually wins the competition is more or less a very successful Premier League club.'

He had a point too. While non-league clubs collected a total of £46,000 for reaching the first round proper, Football League sides would collect just under triple that by progressing through the third round, the stage at which Premier League and Championship clubs are brought into the fold. The question that was being asked was simple. Did they really need the money?

'They [Premier League sides] are fortunate with the money they get. I think the prize money that the men get should be changed and addressed. More money in the earlier rounds would benefit non-league clubs as they go through,' said Potter.

5

The Fifth Tier

LEYTON ORIENT were on the verge of promotion to the Championship in 2014 with only Rotherham United standing in their way. After a good season in League One, Orient had made the play-offs by finishing fourth while their play-off final opponents Rotherham had ended up fifth. Although they had both won an equal number of points, the east Londoners had a superior goal difference which put them above their Yorkshire rivals.

Rotherham had beaten Preston North End in their two-legged semi-final to secure their place at Wembley. Leyton Orient had narrowly beaten Peterborough United with the teams drawing 1-1 at London Road to set up a decisive second leg at Brisbane Road just three days later. Dean Cox and Chris Dagnall scored in the 60th and 88th minutes respectively, helping them through despite a 92nd-minute consolation goal from Conor Washington.

The final was tipped to be a huge occasion for both sides. The O's had narrowly missed out on the play-offs the previous year, with Swindon Town finishing above them in the final play-off spot. Rotherham themselves were enjoying their success, having just been automatically promoted from League Two. Over 43,000 supporters made their way to the biggest stage in English football, Wembley Stadium, to watch the battle for a place in the Championship.

Orient fans were ecstatic with their team having taken a two-goal lead. Moses Odubajo broke the deadlock in the 34th minute when he volleyed the ball into the roof of the net before Adam Collin had realised what hit him. Dean Cox then doubled the lead when he tapped the ball home in the 40th minute before wheeling away in celebration. That joy was short-lived in the second half as Alex Revell scored twice against his former club to spoil the party atmosphere. A miscue from Orient keeper Jamie Jones allowed Revell to poke the ball beyond him, before he lobbed Jones with an audacious effort from distance. The game went to penalties and, once again, Orient took the lead, 3-2. A miss each for Mathieu Baudry and Chris Dagnall allowed James Tavernier and Richard Smallwood to send Rotherham into the Championship and condemn Orient to their fate.

It had taken Barry Hearn 19 years to get the club to the League One play-offs. During the 1998/99 season, Leyton Orient finished sixth in the Third Division – the bottom tier as it was then – and participated in the play-offs alongside Scunthorpe United, Rotherham United and Swansea City. Orient had beaten the Millers 4-2 on penalties, having drawn 0-0 over two legs, but they were defeated 1-0 by Scunthorpe in the final. A couple of years later they found themselves in the play-off final once again. After finishing fifth in the Third Division, Orient went up against Hull City in the semi-final, winning 2-1 after two legs. In the final they faced Blackpool, who had beaten Hartlepool United 5-1 in the other semi-final, and suffered heartbreak as they lost 4-2. The O's had spent a lot of time battling at the bottom of the Third Division following their play-off defeat, finishing 18th and 19th before they reached mid-table in 2004/05.

Hearn's side had finally achieved promotion in the 2005/06 season, ten years after he had bought the club. Having spent 11 years in England's bottom division they gained automatic promotion, finishing third by three points, just behind Carlisle United and Northampton Town. Their promotion saw them spend ten years in League One, but it hadn't been a smooth ride at all. They faced relegation battles twice, finishing 20th in 2006/07 and 2011/12, while they almost reached the play-offs in 2011 but missed out by a point as Bournemouth finished in the final play-off place. On top of a few mid-table finishes too, the club had become comfortable in League One.

When Italian businessman Francesco Becchetti showed an interest in buying Orient, Hearn felt it was the right time to step away. Becchetti seemed to be the perfect fit for Orient as they looked to get out of League One and into the Championship. That wasn't how it panned out though and during the 2014/15 season, they found themselves dropping down the pyramid into League Two. The relegation hadn't been by a huge margin, finishing three points behind 20th place, but they hadn't done enough to save themselves. The following season they almost made the play-offs but finished eighth, six points off AFC Wimbledon in the final play-off spot. With a second season in League Two the wheels had fallen off and after a difficult 2016/17 Orient found themselves relegated from the Football League to the National League. The O's had picked up three wins and a draw in their opening six games but a bad run of form including two runs of six losses on the bounce meant they found themselves rock bottom and 12 points from safety. For a huge club like Orient, it was a massive reality check. A 112-year tenancy in the Football League was over and there was no doubt that the missed opportunity at promotion in 2013/14 played a role in the reversal of fortunes.

'It's always a big disappointment to everyone at the football club. I had a similar experience at Reading and a number of other clubs, and it certainly creates a hangover effect,' said Jobi McAnuff, who had left Orient in 2016 and then re-signed after relegation the following year. 'The following season, that happened to the club. With a new owner, it turned out not to be a successful time.'

The troubled period had begun with the new owner pushing the manager out in the first two months of the season. Many of the play-off players had gone by Christmas while three managers and a sporting director were sacked by the end of the season. The loss in the play-offs had played a role in the fall of Orient, but the continued sackings as well as the talk of players not playing due to unpaid wages and general malaise in the running of the club meant that

Orient were slowly dying. Jobi hadn't been a member of the squad that was relegated from the Football League as he had been released at the end of 2015/16, moving on to Stevenage before returning as Orient prepared for life in the National League.

'After that era, when they did get relegated from the league, I played against them, and it was a team of kids by the end. It was exceedingly difficult with some of those coming through and doing well. In such a tough league, which League Two is, they were still learning and trying to find their feet. It was probably a challenge too far for those, but everyone knew there would need to be a huge rebuild to try and get the club back on track.'

Having spent five years at Reading, including one season in the Premier League, McAnuff joined Orient following the takeover by Becchetti. He had been at Brisbane Road for two years, playing in both League One and League Two, but after a difficult couple of years he felt he had to move away. The second year was particularly difficult as he didn't feature for the side in the first half of 2015/16, which was soon accompanied by stories of interference in the team selection by the chairman.

'Getting away after the couple of years I spent at Orient was about enjoying my football. I managed to do that at Stevenage, and it was an important year in that respect. I knew from my point of view, I hadn't played my best football at the club and to be part of the squad that got relegated [from League One in 2014/15] didn't sit right with me,' he recalled. 'I wasn't given the opportunity to put that right in the next season. I felt there was unfinished business from that and as much as the club hadn't seen the best of me, I don't think I saw the best of Orient.'

The rebuild that was needed began in the National League. Following the O's relegation, Francesco Becchetti decided to sell the club to Nigel Travis, the chairman of Dunkin' Brands, with both him and vice-chairman Kent Teague left to pick up the pieces. They had employed former player and manager Martin Ling as their first order of business, with the new director of football given the task of rebuilding the squad. He wanted to bring McAnuff back to the club and the move from Stevenage to the O's meant he was giving up the Football League for a return to Brisbane Road.

McAnuff said, 'After speaking with Martin Ling, I saw the desire to get me back to the club with the owners gone from the previous regime. They were brilliant in not talking about the past. In their mind, it was very much a clean slate, and I was given the opportunity to show my best self, but the goal to get the club back into the Football League was something I needed in my career. With me getting on with my age, it was good to have that goal and motivation to keep going.'

The first season in the National League was an important one for Orient, especially in their pursuit of reaching League Two once again. They needed to adapt to life in the fifth tier, having been punching above their weight at the top of League One not so long ago. Wolverhampton Wanderers had gone straight back up to the Championship in 2014 while Orient had beaten the likes of Sheffield United and Bristol City to the play-offs. Although they had a strong side at the time, their stature compared to those clubs was lower and, with relegation, Orient had gone full circle.

'It was a learning curve for everyone at the club. Having never played in the National League and visiting some different grounds, it was good to see the different atmospheres. With Leyton Orient being the club it is, it was like a cup final every week. It was a period we needed to adapt. The club were close to going out of business quickly at the end of that disappointing spell under the previous owner and it [the first year] was a good opportunity to stabilise without the real expectation on the team. Many fans would have expected us to go straight back up, but we used it to get to grips with everything and used it as a platform to move forward. At the club, we were looking towards the future,' said McAnuff.

Orient had picked up 16 points in their opening eight games of the season but found themselves in a relegation battle after they went 15 games without a win. Draws against Aldershot Town, Barrow, Wrexham, Dover Athletic and Chester had seen them pick up five points, but ten losses meant they were struggling for form. When Justin Edinburgh was appointed manager at the end of November, Orient's fortune in the league changed. A stabilising season saw them finish 13th as they looked to continue their rebuild and although it wasn't what the fans had expected, for the players, it was exactly what they needed.

'We felt like we were making progress. At the start of the season, we felt like we were going to do okay but then we had a really bad run of form where we couldn't win a game for a long time. Moving towards the second half of the season [when Justin Edinburgh came in], he set a purpose to what we were doing. We weren't a team that was satisfied with it, but we knew it would benefit us the following year,' said McAnuff.

The O's had 24 games under the management of Edinburgh during the 2017/18 season. He led the club on to 11 wins and six draws including good results against sides in the automatic promotion spots and play-off places. Orient drew with Macclesfield Town and Tranmere Rovers, who finished in the top two, as well as with Ebbsfleet United and Boreham Wood, who finished sixth and fourth respectively. They also beat seventh-placed AFC Fylde and third-placed Sutton United. It had given Orient some hope as they prepared for a title-challenging season in the National League.

'He [Edinburgh] brought a winning and no-excuse mentality. We were there to win games and perform. It was very black and white, with all the players understanding their roles, which made us strong. There was a togetherness that brought players, staff and owners together, and Justin was the drive of that. He pushed us in that direction,' McAnuff explained.

Edinburgh had been at several non-league clubs – Fisher Athletic, Grays Athletic and Rushden & Diamonds – prior to moving into the Football League, and his knowledge of the lower levels certainly helped Orient in their quest to escape the National League.

'That's where the experience comes in,' said McAnuff. 'There are times in the National League when you have to roll your sleeves up. It's not always going to be lovely football and there are a number of tough places to go, whether it's because of the stadium or the facilities. Justin had the experience of going to these places and we certainly leaned on that. That little bit of know-how was vital.'

Edinburgh achieved what he and the club set out to do. The second season in the National League saw Leyton Orient lift the title and reach the Football League once again.

'I think the biggest thing was dealing with that expectation where teams would set up against us and knowing how we could break them down. There were lots of games in the first year where we wouldn't be able to find a way to win. There were times when we thought because we played well or dominated a game, it was okay. It was about winning and getting as many points as we could because we wanted to go up. We knew we couldn't afford to slip up, and it was about achieving the consistency needed to win a league,' said McAnuff.

The biggest improvement had come on the pitch. Orient began their season with a 13-game unbeaten run before suffering defeat to Sutton, which didn't derail them as they went on another unbeaten run, nine games this time, although their form got patchier as it continued. They had found the consistency needed and found themselves fighting for the title alongside Salford City and Solihull Moors.

The race was close but the three sides going for the championship couldn't have been any different. Orient were a historic league club who had fallen on hard times and were trying to get back to where they felt they belonged; Salford were a team built from silly money for instant success following the recent majority takeover by the Class of '92 (former Manchester United players Nicky Butt, Ryan Giggs, Gary and Phil Neville, and Paul Scholes, who wanted to own a football club); and Solihull were the perennial non-league strugglers, formed in 2007, who had suddenly benefited from an injection of money and were having their best-ever season.

Salford had been promoted from the National League North at the end of the 2017/18 season, finishing above Harrogate Town by six points. Both Orient and Solihull were in the National League (Step 1), but it Orient had enjoyed a better season. Moors finished 18th, five places below the O's, who knew they needed to use their experience from 2017/18 to their advantage.

McAnuff said, 'There needed to be self-belief and belief in others which we probably developed in that first season. We knew at the end of the season [2017/18], we would be a match for anyone, and it was about adding a few pieces to the puzzle. We were confident in our game plan, but it ended up being a tight race with teams that were trying to achieve the same thing. They were good in their own right, and it was a good challenge because we knew we couldn't slip up. Thankfully, we were able to get over the line.'

The crowning of the champions went right down to the final day. Orient travelled to Solihull in the penultimate game of the season but after a stalemate between the two sides, the O's needed a single point to beat their rivals to the title. Orient welcomed Braintree Town to Brisbane Road, knowing a draw would be enough, but it was never going to be easy and although their opponents were in the relegation zone, the destination of the title sat in Orient's control.

'Leading into the game, the nerves were there,' explained McAnuff. 'We knew it was in our hands but sometimes that is not a nice feeling to have. A bad performance and result would have taken that away from us. The fact that we weren't over the line, always sat in the back of our minds and the last thing we wanted to do was mess it up. There had been too much hard work put in.

'The fans felt the same way as us. You could feel the nervousness in the crowd. There was that anticipation mixed with excitement and a bit of hope we can do it. It was great to be at home on the final day. You think about achieving these things and to do it at home, in front of our fans, was the icing on the cake. The fans who made all the journeys, that probably wouldn't have in previous years, and our home support had been incredible throughout the season. If you are going to write a script, that's what you would put [home fans being there to share the moment].'

The game against Braintree finished 0-0. It wasn't the star-studded performance Orient had hoped for against a relegated side, but it was enough and that was all that mattered. As the referee went to blow the whistle, fans waited. With the additional three minutes played, the ball was launched up the field and the referee brought the game to an end. Players and fans ran on the field to celebrate promotion back to the Football League.

* * *

On Saturday, 4 May 2019, Notts County were relegated from the Football League. Their nightmare had become a reality after finding themselves bottom of League Two during the 2018/19 season, but no one expected it to happen. At the start of the season the Magpies had ambitions of reaching League One, but after a poor start, their aim soon changed as they sought to avoid relegation rather than fighting at the top.

'It was a huge shock,' said Notts County's media manager, Nick Richardson. 'When we went into the season, we had a target of challenging for a place in League One. We had two managers early in the season before Neal Ardley came in to steer the ship. He couldn't save us, and we were relegated on the last day at Swindon Town. It was a horrible day for everyone at the club. It brought an end to our brand and identity of being the oldest professional football league club [in the world] and that was what made us special. From what we expected, it was really sad. The club had been up for sale for almost a year, and we faced a lot of uncertainty. It was a dark time to be involved with the club.'

The season had begun with a draw at home to Colchester United but a run of six losses on the spin put Notts in the relegation zone. The poor run of form had seen the first managerial casualty of the season as Kevin Nolan was relieved of his duties, with Harry Kewell taking over. Under Kewell, after losing in his first two games, County went on a five-game unbeaten run, drawing 3-3 with Stevenage and 0-0 with Northampton Town before they beat Crewe Alexandra to record their first win of the season, adding to that with victories over Crawley Town and Macclesfield Town. Their form had improved but three further losses and two draws weren't enough to keep Kewell in his job. He had briefly lifted Notts out of the relegation zone, although they remained hovering above it, but sitting 22nd was not a comfortable position for the Magpies and as a result they looked to bring in a manager who could divert them away from the dreaded drop.

Ardley was appointed at the end of November as County hoped he could be the one to keep them up. His first game was a 2-0 loss to Mansfield Town before Tranmere were defeated at Meadow Lane the following week. Under Ardley, Notts struggled for form. After his first win they could only manage two more in the ten games that followed as they were rooted to the bottom of the League Two table. As the season neared its end, County shuffled between bottom and second-bottom with a lingering hope of escaping the clutches of relegation.

The penultimate game of the season saw County defeat Grimsby Town at home, giving them a chance at avoiding following already-relegated Yeovil Town out of the Football League. Notts faced a tough test against Swindon Town and desperately needed to win, while also hoping that Macclesfield slipped up at Cambridge United.

Swindon looked more like scoring but it was the County fans who were celebrating the opening goal. Top scorer Kane Hemmings had put them ahead from the penalty spot in the 51st minute, while elsewhere Macclesfield were losing to Cambridge. There was some hope for the Magpies as the match progressed, but their spirit was dampened when Kaiyne Woolery brought Swindon level with 20 minutes to play. Notts believed they could still pull off the great escape until Theo Robinson put the hosts ahead five minutes later. As it stood, they were going down, and any hope of the great escape the supporters thought they would witness was ended when Robinson completed his brace in the 92nd minute. The once-mighty Notts County were now the biggest fish in the National League Ocean.

The relegation wasn't just contributed to on the pitch. The club had been up for sale for a long time and it was hard to see an end to the ordeal. A buyer was desperately needed to stabilise the club so the players could focus on getting back to the Football League. 'There were a string of issues for the owner [Alan Hardy] at the time. Everyone probably knows about his tweet of an inappropriate photo, and it was the same day he put the club up for sale. He told us he needed to sell to focus on his external business – Paragon Interiors – which was struggling. He wanted to focus on saving that so I wouldn't say he was giving up on a failing club. It was more about his circumstances at the time that led to the decision [to sell the club],' said Richardson.

The problems Notts County faced had begun almost ten years prior to relegation to the National League. The club had narrowly survived the drop in 2013/14, but there had been bigger problems in 2009/10. A takeover had brought a lot of hope to the County supporters, with the club searching to reach the highest level in the English game in the coming years. Although County went up as League Two champions in 2009/10, that achievement masked what had happened off the pitch, with the takeover quickly unravelling and the club surviving two winding-up petitions from HMRC.

'There was a takeover by Munto [Finance], who came along and were supposedly millionaires. I believe that's where the problems started but they didn't come to surface until later on because what came with them was the signings of Kasper Schmeichel, Sol Campbell and Lee Hughes,' said County's all-time record goalscorer, Les Bradd. 'When players like that come on board, people start to take notice and people think we are going places. The Munto questions had disappeared. That season, the club were promoted to League One, but the manager had departed at the end of the season [Steve Cotterill had taken over in February, following a caretaker spell by Dave Kevan, after a stint under Hanse Bakke with Ian McParland having started the season in charge – Kevan and Michael Johnson also had joint caretaker charge between McParland and Bakke].'

On 14 July 2009, the club were brought by Munto Finance, controlled by Qadbak Investments, with Peter

Trembling, a representative for the company, being named chairman. It had seemed like a huge opportunity for Notts County as they sought to rise up the leagues. Ex-England manager Sven-Göran Eriksson was brought on board as the Director of Football along with the huge signing of a young Kasper Schmeichel from Manchester City.

The 2009/10 season had got off to a great start for County as they won 5-0 against Bradford City (with Lee Hughes scoring his first hat-trick for the club) and 4-0 away to Macclesfield. The third game of the season had ended in a 2-1 defeat away to Chesterfield but that was put out of mind against Dagenham & Redbridge as they beat the Daggers 3-0 at Meadow Lane. With the Magpies sitting towards the top end of the table, the squad was boosted just three days later when Notts signed former England international Sol Campbell, who had committed himself to five years in Nottingham.

The Magpies' away form stuttered their progress on the pitch and they were narrowly beaten 1-0 by Barnet before they could only manage a point against Burton Albion. Although they had hit five past Northampton Town in the next game as Matt Ritchie scored a brace and Hughes netted three, a third loss of the season came at Morecambe.

Behind the scenes, there were more problems. A month after signing Campbell, his contract was ended as he walked out, having appeared only once, in that defeat at Morecambe. Notts then embarked on a nine-game unbeaten run, before a fourth loss of the season arrived at Rochdale. The games that followed saw the Magpies pick up another six points, beating Darlington and Hereford United and keeping two cleans sheets in the process.

The squad had been doing well on the pitch but the problems in the boardroom had kept the media's eye on the club for the wrong reasons. Munto had decided to sell up, Peter Trembling taking ownership for a nominal fee. With a sense of stability after Trembling's takeover, Notts were able to focus on the pitch and recorded another four wins: beating Burton Albion, Darlington, Barnet and Grimsby Town.

A trip to Eddie Howe's Bournemouth ended in yet another defeat on the road, but more importantly, the club had been sold once again as Ray Trew had become the third owner in the space of a season, but that hadn't stopped County on the pitch as they marched towards the League Two title. They recorded their longest unbeaten run of the season, 16 games, securing their promotion to League One on Saturday, 17 April 2010 and wrapping up the championship with a 5-0 thrashing over already-relegated Darlington ten days later.

Continued managerial instability didn't help for Notts as they settled into League One. After undergoing four changes in the dugout in 2009/10, they had clinched the championship under Steve Cotterill, but he departed at the end of the season and was replaced by Craig Short. The former County player had spent a year at Hungarian side Ferencváros before being appointed by the Magpies. Short had a tough start and only 18 games after taking over, with eight wins and nine defeats, he was sacked and replaced by former MK Dons and Blackburn manager Paul Ince. Ince was in charge for the majority of the remainder of the season, leading the team 29 times, but a run of defeats on the spin after an inconsistent spell meant he became the next casualty.

County remained managerless for a further two defeats before Martin Allen was brought in. The final five games of the season saw Allen win two, draw two and lose one, but more importantly, Notts County had stayed up by three points despite finding themselves in the relegation zone four times over the course of the season.

The 2011/12 season was a lot better for Notts, who started well under Allen, although a poor run of form and a drop into mid-table cost Allen his job with 16 games of the season left. Keith Curle was his replacement and under new management the Magpies ended up finishing seventh, missing out on the final play-off spot to Stevenage only on goal difference.

Curle didn't see out the following season and was replaced in February by Chris Kiwomya, who led Notts to a mid-table finish, but he only lasted in his position until October 2013 and was replaced by former Meadow Lane favourite Shaun Derry whose task was to ensure the Magpies remained in League One. It was a difficult campaign but six wins in the final nine games arrived at just the right time, and a final-day draw at Oldham Athletic was enough to secure survival despite sitting in the relegation zone with two matches left.

'Nearly 5,000 County fans made the trip to Oldham,' explained Bradd. 'We had avoided relegation by the skin of our teeth and needed to improve going into the next season. That didn't happen and we were relegated [from League One]. Recruitment had been taken out of the manager's hands and he wasn't necessarily given the players he wanted. It was a spiral from that point, and it seemed to continue towards 2017.'

Derry remained in charge for the majority of the 2014/15 season but by the time of his departure in March 2015, relegation back to the bottom tier looked likely. A brief spell of three defeats under caretakers Paul Hart and Mick Halsall was followed by the appointment of Dutchman Ricardo Moniz, but he couldn't stop the rot and was out of a job by December with the Magpies struggling in League Two.

Notts flirted with the relegation zone under Moniz, then Jamie Fullarton and latterly Mark Cooper in 2015/16, and were stuck in the bottom half again under John Sheridan and then Kevin Nolan the following year, but in Nolan's sole full season in charge – 2017/18 – they came close to going back up.

Nolan's team finished fifth but were beaten over two legs in the semi-finals by Coventry City, who then went on to beat Exeter City in the final at Wembley, and by November 2018 Nolan was gone with Notts on their way to relegation out of the Football League for the first time in their history. A short spell with Harry Kewell in charge proved a disaster and then Neal Ardley wasn't able to arrest the slide.

County struggled to adapt in the National League but once they did they established themselves as contenders for an immediate return to League Two, sitting third after 38 games by the time Covid-19 caused the suspension of the season in March 2020. The halt had come at the worst time for Notts after four wins in succession, including against leaders Barrow.

National League clubs opted in April to end the season with immediate effect but a solution on promotion and relegation wasn't decided until June. After another vote among member clubs, the final decision was to promote based on a points-per-game average and as a result, Barrow had been declared champions on 17 June, having held a four-point lead over Harrogate after playing the same number of games. The title triumph had pushed the Bluebirds into League Two with a points average of 1.89, enough to see them climb the ladder into the Football League for the first time in 48 years. While the only automatic promotion place had been filled, Harrogate, Notts County, Yeovil, Boreham Wood, Halifax, and Barnet made the play-offs. For County, it was a good end to the season as they sought to rise back to League Two at their first attempt.

'We wanted to finish the season above anything else,' explained Nick Richardson. 'We didn't want a null and void decision because there had been a lot of work and the majority of the season had been played. Some teams missed out on points-per-game, but we felt that was the best decision at the time and, thankfully, we made the play-offs based on that.'

The PPG solution meant Barnet had crept into the play-offs. Harrogate, Notts, Yeovil, Boreham Wood and Halifax remained where they had been when the season was ended, but Stockport County had been sitting seventh with Solihull Moors, Hartlepool United and Woking all above Barnet. The Bees had played 35 games compared to the 37, 38 or 39 of the others, giving them a points average of 1.54, enough to finish above Stockport in the final play-off spot. While the decision had been music to the ears of Barnet, it was harsh on Stockport and those below.

With the play-offs given the go-ahead, the teams were forced to compete behind closed doors, leaving stadiums empty and the matches watched from TV screens around the country. The empty grounds were part of numerous Covid-secure rules that clubs had to adhere to.

Richardson said, 'It's one thing to train as a group but it's another for players training away from the group. When we came back in, there were plenty of Covid protocols. Phase one was training in small groups before phase two allowed players to mark each other on the training pitch. You also had the players having to travel to training separately to avoid close contact whilst the training ground became a maze of one-way systems. It was a huge adaptation just for the play-offs and it was like going into the unknown. The players had suffered a longer lay-off than a standard pre-season, so it was tough to get them back up to full fitness for the resumption of competitive football, but we were glad to finish the season.'

The play-off structure saw seven teams involved. As Harrogate and Notts had finished second and third respectively, they automatically qualified for the play-off semi-finals with Yeovil, Boreham Wood, Halifax and Barnet each battling it out in a quarter-final to decide who'd make up the numbers in the semis. Boreham Wood hosted Halifax, winning 2-1 on 17 July before, a day later, the Bees had travelled to Yeovil and were victorious 2-0. Boreham Wood then faced Harrogate, and it was the latter who booked their date at Wembley by winning 1-0, before later in the day County joined them after Kristian Dennis and Callum Roberts had given them a 2-0 win over Barnet.

The final was also played behind closed doors, the new normal of the strange times. Both sides would have loved to have taken their fans to Wembley, but on the pitch, they had a job to do. County were on the back foot early on as Sam Slocombe was made to scramble as a clearance deflected off a Harrogate forward and towards goal. A few minutes later, they found themselves 1-0 down as George Thompson got ahead of the defence and poked the ball beyond the keeper. Aaron Martin missed a golden opportunity for Harrogate but a second goal arrived after 28 minutes as Connor Hall tapped home a cross by Thompson. It had almost gone from bad to worse for County as Martin smashed the ball against the post.

The second half began brightly for County as, within the opening minutes, Roberts fired a free kick beyond Belshaw. The goal back had acted like a catalyst for the Magpies as ten minutes later Roberts was almost a hero, charging through the middle of the pitch but seeing his effort go inches wide of the post from the edge of the box, and a through ball to Wootton was saved at the near post by Belshaw. But the fourth goal of the game went to Harrogate as Jack Diamond flicked a cross into the far corner with just under 20 minutes to play. Wes Thomas was denied by a point-blank save by Belshaw before Michael Doyle had a shot blocked, but Harrogate marched into League Two for the first time in their history.

It was disappointing for County not to be promoted back to the EFL on their first attempt, but for the club, it was a good season. Pundits and neutrals speculated it was a surprise to see County in the play-offs at all, but Nick Richardson didn't agree. He was also unsure whether Notts' play-off campaign would have been different had they been able to welcome supporters to their games.

'I'd say it would be far-fetched to call it a surprise,' he said. 'Many expected us to compete at the top of the league, but from the takeover process, it was an amazing achievement to finish third. We also reached the semi-final of the FA Trophy, which was great. A week before the season, the takeover happened which meant we were able to bring in players. Neal [Ardley] got us firing by Christmas, and before the lockdown, we were even tipped to beat Barrow to the title. For us, it was a good first season.

'It was tough to say [whether having no fans affected the players]. You could speculate but the fact is that it affects some more than others. We are the best-supported team in the league, averaging 1,000 more than any other club. That's a disadvantage to us as the fans really get behind us.

We are also the best-supported team on the road so you could say we have been affected more than most.'

Ardley remained in charge ahead of the 2020/21 season and led County through most of it before being sacked in March 2021 with the team a long way adrift of leaders and eventual champions Sutton United. Notts eventually finished fifth, missing out on an automatic play-off semi-final, but they got past Chesterfield in their quarter-final thanks to a 3-2 victory at Meadow Lane, only to lose 4-2 after extra time at Torquay United in the semi, suffering play-off heartbreak once again.

6

True Blue

IPSWICH TOWN Women found themselves drawn against Women's Super League side Manchester City in the 2019/20 FA Women's Cup. The Tractor Girls had navigated their way through several rounds by beating Royston Town, Norwich City, AFC Basildon, Chichester City, Portsmouth, and Huddersfield Town before being rewarded with the tie of a lifetime.

The journey for Ipswich had begun in the second qualifying round as they were drawn against Eastern Region Women's Football League side Royston. The Crows were a level below Ipswich, but the Tractor Girls had to stay focused on the task in hand if they were going to make it through.

Although they had only taken a 2-0 lead into the half-time break, with goals from Maddie Biggs and Eloise King, a further five goals in the second half from King, Biggs, Lindsey Cooper and a double from Amanda Crump helped them on to a huge 7-0 win.

The big victories didn't end there though as the Blues eased past their East Anglian rivals Norwich City, winning 6-1, while they scored a further 11 goals against Basildon and Chichester, winning 5-0 and 6-0 respectively. The victories had made their incredible run seem easy, but Royston were their only lower-league opponents; Norwich and Basildon were in the same division as Ipswich, the FA Women's National League Division One South East, while Chichester could be found in the Southern Premier Division, the league above.

'We had played six games in the cup before being drawn against City,' said manager Joe Sheehan. 'We hadn't done anything differently and treated every game like we would when playing in the league. We needed to do what we did best, whether that was against teams in the league above or below. We managed to play pretty well in each round and progress through the competition.'

After getting beyond Chichester in the second round proper, Town found themselves facing another tough game against a side in the league above, Portsmouth. Pompey hadn't been doing brilliantly in the Southern Premier Division, eventually winning five of the nine games they played during the 2019/20 season, but Ipswich still found it tough. Paige Peake's free kick was enough to send them into the fourth round proper, setting up a tie with Huddersfield who had only progressed through two rounds themselves. The tier-three side had begun their run in the second round proper, edging past Stoke City on penalties after a 1-1 draw, before they narrowly beat Loughborough Foxes on the road.

The fourth-round tie was expected to be closer than it actually was, but Ipswich continued their goalscoring form as they netted four against the Terriers. Biggs scored three of those in the first half as she punished poor defending from the hosts, before Natasha Thomas also scored to seal the win at the John Smith's Stadium.

The impressive run had to come to an end, however, and it did in the fifth round after a 10-0 defeat to Manchester City. The strength of the Women's Super League side had proven too much for tier-four Ipswich as Pauline Bremer, Jess Park and Georgia Stanway all scored hat-tricks while Laura Coombs also contributed a goal. It would have taken an almighty effort for Ipswich to beat a Super League side but despite the loss, Sheehan was happy with the adventure they had been on. What made it even sweeter was that they had made history by progressing as far as they did.

'It was brilliant and a great experience for us. It's the furthest a tier-four side has ever gone in the history of the competition so that made us even prouder. We fielded a team [in the City game] which started with eight players who were under 18, which was remarkable.'

Drawing the calibre of opponent they did meant they had the opportunity to play in the Academy Stadium, a 7,000-seater facility on Manchester City's Etihad Campus, against some of the world's best players and internationals. City had started with the likes of captain Steph Houghton, Kiera Walsh and Demi Stokes, showing a certain respect to Ipswich.

'These players [who started for Ipswich] have played for their counties in their respective age groups, but it doesn't compare to senior internationals. To compete against one of the best teams in the world, in a nice stadium and in front of thousands [including 500 travelling fans] was fantastic,' said Sheehan.

Ipswich knew it would be one of the toughest games of their lives and certainly didn't expect to get a positive result. A win or draw, or personal accolades, would have been a pure bonus, but all they could do was make themselves and their families proud as they stepped out on to the pitch in what for many of the players would have been a once-in-a-lifetime opportunity.

Sheehan said, 'It was a difficult game, but we always knew that. We knew we'd be up against players who are considered world-class, but we still tried to implement our game plan, knowing we'd have limited chances. We wanted to try and get something from the game, because there would have been no point going if we didn't want to compete. Being faced against these type of players was a good challenge, and it gave us a good indication of the standard we will be looking to reach in the future.'

Although Ipswich's run in the FA Women's Cup had come to an end, they were flying in the league. They were on the quest for promotion to the FA Women's National League Southern Premier Division and sat top of their division, just a point ahead of AFC Wimbledon Ladies. The Tractor Girls had played the same number of games as their title rivals but had recorded one more victory, keeping them just ahead of the Dons, while an extra 23 goals scored acted as an extra point. Spoils shared between the sides and the reverse fixture being played meant neither side could take any more points off each other.

'It [the league] ended up being tougher than we had imagined. Although it was our own doing, I never really felt there were teams in the league that could match us. It was more a case of doing what we need to do, and we had a good run up until Christmas,' Sheehan recalled. 'We had drawn on the opening day with Wimbledon but felt we should have beaten them after a good performance. When they beat us in January [Ipswich's only defeat at the time], it was a freak result.'

Ipswich were on course for another victory in the reverse fixture against Wimbledon but were caught short as they lost from a winning position. It reflected the competition that the Blues faced as they battled for promotion. As results went against Ipswich, their title rivals had slowly moved up the table and soon found themselves one point behind the Tractor Girls.

Sheehan explained, 'We were completely cruising until injury time when we got caught with two sucker punches and goals that were certainly freak goals. Wimbledon seemed to have crept up on us whilst we suffered a defeat to Enfield Town. That was another game we dominated but, to be fair to them, they put in an organised performance which saw them contain us for as long as they could before getting rewarded from some counterattacks.'

The title race had become closer than Sheehan had expected but his belief in his side to go on and win the league was still there. The defeats they had suffered were minor setbacks, but more importantly, they were still top, having played the Dons twice.

Sheehan continued, 'The losses we faced were down to us causing our own problems and not being clinical enough in front of goal. We were in a strong position because [fourth-placed] Billericay hadn't played Wimbledon at all. A lot of the teams below us hadn't played both so although we were top by a point, we had a significant goal difference and other sides had to play each other. They were bound to drop points.'

Sheehan hadn't been Ipswich's manager for long, joining towards the end of the 2018/19 season. Although he had spent just over a year in the role, his time at the club had spanned a longer period as he had been the lead coach of the Women's Regional Under-21 Academy team from October 2017.

He said, 'I was already employed at the club full-time. I was employed to oversee and put together an academy side to play in the WSL Academy League, so it was a huge project. Once we got the academy going, we managed to build it into a strong one.'

The FA had set up a new initiative which included the creation of a regional elite programme. It meant Ipswich's academy team had been given a unique opportunity to play against the academy sides of the Women's Super League, despite their first team not being in the WSL.

The 2019/20 season had seen all bar newly promoted Tottenham Hotspur enter an academy side into the league while Ipswich were the only non-WSL club to have entered a team themselves.

The 2018/19 season was the first for Ipswich in the WSL Academy League as they entered under the name of FA East Region, finishing ninth ahead of the academies of Birmingham City Women and Yeovil Town Ladies. They had also reached the League Cup semi-final with wins over ECFA National Team and Manchester City Academy but were defeated in the semi-finals by Arsenal. They improved the following season, sitting sixth, but with the league campaign being cut short they didn't get the chance to improve their position. They had also reached the semi-final of the League Cup for the second year in a row, getting past Tottenham Hotspur and Reading Academy, but with another season ended early, their clash with Durham was postponed indefinitely. The work of the club meant they had produced a very competitive youth setup that allowed players to progress to the first team.

Sheehan's decision to take over the first team was one that benefited both sides. He felt there was no point having a decent academy setup if there was no route into the first team. The pathway between the two sides was an essential part of the process and, by taking over as first-team manager, he was in a position to make that happen.

'When I made the step up, it was about giving a path of progression to the girls, but the team was still a very grassroots side and the women's game had progressed across the country. We needed to bridge the gap whilst trying to create a professional outfit,' Sheehan said.

The biggest target was off the pitch as they looked to turn a grassroots women's side into a professional team that could reach the Women's Super League, but the magnitude of the task meant it wouldn't be easy. The time and resources needed to achieve this were enough in themselves as Ipswich also had to put together an off-field staff group who could give the club a professional feel while achieving their goals on the pitch. The relationship they had with the men's side certainly helped that cause.

Sheehan said, 'It's a great relationship we have. My assistant and I are full-time and based at the men's first-team training ground [Playford Road]. The benefit of the relationship allows us to be in a professional environment and that really helps. We've had [men's first-team manager] Paul Lambert attend our games, even our FA Women's Cup tie in Manchester. We get to use all the facilities which are of an exceptionally good standard, and we fall under the club's umbrella, so the environment it brings is excellent. We have a great relationship with all the staff to help and support what we want to do.'

The Ipswich boss was confident in his side's ability to reach the next level, taking them one division off the second tier, the Women's Championship. He had expected the 2020/21 season to be tough but their results on the pitch boosted his confidence.

The club had come a long way after finishing seventh in the 2013/14 South East Combination Women's Football

League. When the restructure to the women's football pyramid had seen tier four become the Women's Premier League Division One, there was very little consistency when it came to league positions for the Tractor Girls. After finishing fifth during the following season, they dropped down to their lowest league position, ninth in 2016/17, but were never really in danger of relegation before they finished third in 2017/18.

They couldn't build on their top-three finish as the Blues dropped down to seventh in 2018/19. The Women's Premier League had been rebranded again, becoming the FA Women's National League, with Town competing in the Division One South East. The season had been a great stabilising season for Sheehan before he propelled the club to the heights they sought, sitting top of the league in 2019/20.

He said, 'We felt we were in a good position despite the couple of blips we had. We were confident we could win enough games towards the end of the season to get the title. Not much was needed to be done [to improve the setup we had]. It's about experience and we will always try to continue our development as a squad and improve. That has been shown on the pitch.'

When Sheehan looked at the improvement they had made, the matches against Huddersfield and Portsmouth in the FA Cup as well as their 2019/20 pre-season friendly against Nottingham Forest Women came to mind. The friendly had seen the Tractor Girls beat National League Northern Premier Division side Forest 3-1 on the road before achieving their exploits in the cup.

Sheehan said, 'In those games [against sides in the league above], we won pretty comfortably. Although one was a pre-season game, it showed how far the club had come and gave us an idea of what life could be like if we were to achieve promotion.'

The National League wasn't a competition Ipswich wanted to stay in and was merely a stepping stone as they sought to chase their dreams. The club had ambitions of reaching the very top level of women's football, while Sheehan also wanted the chance to manage at that level.

'I want to manage at the top level. I'm ambitious about it and confident I'll get the chance to do so in my career. I want to do it with the club I'm currently at as the goal for both myself and the club is to reach the Women's Super League,' he said.

7

Mind the Gap

THOSE WHO found their way to Market Road had the little-known world of the London Underground Football League unveiled before their very eyes.

'The league seems to be known by a select few,' said District Line Railway player-manager Jason Alex Hill. 'We are trying to use the power of social media as a platform to help amplify the league as we want spectators to have an awareness and interest in the league. While we want to improve spectator numbers at our games, we also hope to find ways of getting additional funding to help expand the league. I'd love to see more teams playing within our league.'

The story behind the London Underground Football League was simple. It was after a successful knockout tournament in 1995, in which District Line had won 2-1 against Piccadilly, that the idea had come about. The league was created a year later by Andy Anthony, with the help of Chris Leach, to add structure to the teams already competing at the time. Transport for London owned a lot of land in London, including a sports facility in Acton where teams all over the network used to get together and play, but its use had been withdrawn before a negotiation to organise funds to allow those sides to continue playing.

'A league was created to bring staff together from departments of Transport for London and to encourage socialisation and healthy activity. Over the 25 years the league has been operating, it has grown in popularity and the standard has improved,' said Hill.

The league was completed by several recognisable underground lines, with the Hammersmith & City, Northern, Metropolitan, Elizabeth, Waterloo & City, and the Jubilee line competing alongside the District line, Piccadilly line and London Overground, while Tubelines, the management company for maintenance of the network, and the British Transport Police also competed. The Bakerloo, Victoria and Central lines were involved as recently as the 2018/19 season, but for different reasons they pulled their squads from the league and have not taken part since.

Initially, the league had been a single division but three seasons after its formation, in order to make it more competitive and with the increasing number of teams, it was split into two divisions to allow for promotion and relegation for the 1999/00 season. The two divisions was something the teams preferred, but it was only changed after it was found that some sides were far stronger than others, meaning the same teams would be fighting at the top. Adding a second division allowed the slightly weaker teams a fairer chance to compete, growing at their own pace.

'The bottom two sides in Division One are relegated and their place taken by the top two teams in Division Two via automatic promotion,' Hill explained. 'We don't have play-offs, but we do have a couple of cup competitions to have another chance at winning silverware.'

Piccadilly manager Cem Toygar is one of those who preferred the two-division system.

'I like two divisions as opposed to one,' he said. 'It gives teams more of an incentive to achieve greater things and be competitive all season as they battle for promotion and against relegation, respectively. It makes the league more exciting. I'd even have a third division with several teams on the waiting list [to join the league] but the budget we have wouldn't allow for that unless we received a generous sponsor in the future.'

The expansion of the league required additional teams joining, something Toygar was all for. The Bakerloo and Victoria lines were sides that had competed before but sat on the waiting list for the 2020/21 season, hoping they'd be competing once again. He knew that any expansion would require more funding, but this was impossible to come across. The teams were made up of those who worked on the Underground, but they were able to fund the league from their own pocket alone and it was near impossible to get the funding direct from TFL. Instead, they had hoped to attract a benefactor or huge sponsor to support the league and inject some cash which could've seen another division added if more teams were able to join.

'I'd love to see additional teams joining the league,' said the Piccadilly boss. 'It would add to the competitiveness of the game but also have the entire network represented. On top of other Underground lines, I'd love to see a tram, DLR or bus team involved too.'

Piccadilly FC and District Line Railway AFC were both founding members of the league, but both found themselves in different divisions. District Line had been one of the strongest and most successful sides in the history of the league, claiming 21 honours compared to Victoria line's 12 trophies and Piccadilly's seven, but troubles faced off the field saw them relegated to Division Two. Manager Hill knew how important it was to get his side back into the top division and competing for the title once again. Stabilising the club off the pitch had been the focus, but once that was achieved the focus turned to fighting for promotion with the hope they would finally get promoted at the end of the 2019/20 season.

'As a Division Two team on the cusp of promotion, we have a strong enough squad with some real quality that would easily match and beat some of those sides in the top division,' said Hill. 'I think District Line is one of the biggest clubs in the league, winning most of the silverware since its inception in 1996. In more recent times, 2017 in particular, we found it to be a tough time for the club. The manager at the time retired and a lot of the players who had been together for nearly 20 years decided to leave the club as well. Consequently, the team struggled and were relegated that season. I came in as player-manager to try and resurrect the team.'

Between 2009 and 2014, District Line Railway had won five Division One titles in a row but from 2017 onwards they hadn't tasted success as other sides progressed while they rebuilt from scratch. The 2018/19 season had seen them finish third behind Hammersmith & City Line FC and Northern Line FC as they sought promotion back to the top division. A season later they had improved drastically, finding themselves top of Division Two before the season was halted. Although the season had been suspended indefinitely, it wasn't classified as null and void. Instead, as an independent league, when the pitches became available and the government allowed competitive sport to resume, it could be completed. The majority of clubs had played all of their games but with a few loose ends to tie up, the remaining matches needed to be completed.

Piccadilly FC had also struggled before Toygar took over. He had been a fringe player for Piccadilly after working on the line for several years, but after he saw the troubles the club faced he decided to take over as chairman, helping to keep the team going and ensuring they remained on course to be the best in the league.

He explained, 'I used to work at Russell Square, and I was on the team as a fringe player for years. I've always had a soft spot for the Piccadilly line and the Northern line as I am a north London guy. I've always lived between Archway and Highgate for most of my years too. When Piccadilly were relegated during the 2014/15 season and almost folded with such a small squad due to players not showing up at games, I didn't want to see the team fold and had a vision to make them a great team again. It had taken me three seasons to get them back to Division One, but we have won the Division One title in the last two seasons. Before that, the last and only time we had won it before was during the 2002/03 season.'

Although District Line had found themselves further down than they had hoped, they still kept an eye on their biggest rivals, Piccadilly, who had found themselves top of Division One and won their second consecutive championship. A competitive league was always going to cause rivalries both on and off the pitch, but the rivalry they had with Piccadilly had stemmed from the very first knockout tournament. For Hill, who had previously been on the other side, he had always wanted to beat them.

'We have built some good rivalries. In more recent times, we still see Piccadilly as our main rival despite finding ourselves in different divisions, with both teams starting the league back in the late 90s. Piccadilly struggled during our glory years, but they've grown into a good team, winning Division One back to back. I spent some time playing for the enemy so my personal rivalry stems from there.'

The rivalry swung the other way, but for Piccadilly, Tubelines were also a rival. With the absence of District Line from Division One, Toygar felt they needed to find a rival in their own division to up the importance of the season.

He said, 'Our main rival in the last two seasons has been Tubelines. They're currently our bogey team and have always stepped up against us, but they have also provided a title challenge in the absence of the District Line team.'

The league offered those who loved to play football the chance to do so while working around their shift patterns. Like teams in the emergency services leagues, shift patterns often meant players wouldn't always be available for games and with thousands of people working on the Underground, the teams tended to have large squads that ensured a good number of players would be available for each matchday. This also meant everyone had a fair chance to be involved with the squad and play rather than the same side being fielded each week.

Hill said, 'At District Line we have a squad of 35 players. Having a large squad helps with the shift work that players have to combat so it tends to balance out. During the season, we have already used over 30 players over the course of the season, so it has been very helpful.'

When the league was first created, players had to play for the line they worked on but with the constant movement of drivers across the network and the popularity of the competition, a rule change was made to allow players to play for any team as long as normal transfer and registration rules were followed. It was a rule that had divided opinion among teams in the league, but with sides still struggling for players, it had mainly been seen as a huge positive.

'Years ago, players were tied to the lines they worked on. With the nature of the job these days, employees often moved between departments, so the rule was abolished,' Hill explained. 'The lack of teams is more to do with the budget than anything else. The majority of our finances goes directly into the pitches, and it doesn't come cheap. We don't own the land or the pitch anymore, so we have to block-book them in order to play for the season and some teams that found a decline in players still struggle for numbers now.'

The lack of teams in the league meant transfers were often frequent. Signings didn't require a particular window, but they still needed to be authorised by both clubs. The rule was one that aligned with non-league, with the only difference being the timeframe. Non-league sides need to register their players ahead of a deadline before a game, but this didn't apply to the London Underground League. Instead, they could be signed anytime and be available for the next fixture.

'Both managers have to write to the committee to agree a transfer of players between clubs. Once a transfer is agreed, the squad files are updated. There is no time limit on transfers, and they tend to happen straight away, but I'd like to see them completed at least 48 hours before a game. That makes it fairer in my opinion,' said Hill.

With popularity increasing among groundhoppers, the London Underground League is a recognised competition in its own right but still seemed distant from any other non-league or grassroots league. The structure and detachment only allowed for movement between the two divisions, but this didn't stop Jason dreaming of trying to achieve the same as Met Police FC. Met Police had once consisted of staff from the Metropolitan Police Force before the rule was changed as the commissioner had refused to sanction time off to play for the club. The side had formed in 1919, playing friendlies for nine years before they joined Division One East of the Spartan League in 1928. Since then they have progressed through the non-league pyramid, finding themselves in the Southern League Premier Division South (Step 3). While Met Police have been a huge inspiration to the clubs in the league, others like Hackney Wick, in the Eastern Counties League, came to mind for Hill.

'It's something we've considered [as a club], especially with what Hackney Wick had done with starting from the bottom, but our foundations to achieve the same are still way off. We don't have the financial clout or playing standard to compete just yet, but it is something that we'd like to be part of, whether that's with District Line or another team.

'The main focus right now is to win silverware with District Line and the fantastic group of lads we have on the team. Apart from that, I'd love to be able to grow the team and look at the possibility of entering into other leagues and cup competitions while a women's side is also something I want to see.

'Being from south London, Tooting & Mitcham United were my team. I now live out west and have been to a few games, watching Staines Town, Ashford Town, Hampton & Richmond Borough and my favoured Walton Casuals. I just love the authenticity of it [non-league]. The crowds you see have a real passion for the game and I've met some great people. The players and club officials interact with the paying supporters more also than you'd see at higher levels and I've enjoyed some of the grounds I have visited, with many carrying a real charm with them.'

The same thought of joining the National League System had also crossed the mind of Cem Toygar. He was an avid viewer of non-league football himself and looked towards many of the clubs he had seen for inspiration for the future of Piccadilly FC. While watching the lower leagues, Toygar had also volunteered at a club which had given him a taste of what it could be like.

'I'd love to be involved in non-league,' he said. 'But it would mean we would have to leave the London Underground League. There are regulations and more money needed to run and sustain a club like that. If it were a possibility, I definitely wouldn't dismiss it.

'I am a big fan of Dunstable Town, who I had volunteered for in the past. They helped me to gain some knowledge and understanding of the organisation needed to run a club and how to approach local businesses for sponsorships. I also love Caversham United. They are always interactive with their fans on social media, showing how important it could be for the growth of the club.'

* * *

Ahead of the 2020/21 season, South Western Railway FC were the latest team to join the London Underground League. Following on from their formation in 2019, they had played in the Railway & Corporate Friendly Flexi

Football League, an 11-a-side competition for the travel and transport industries, but ahead of the new season Darren Fielding fancied a change of scenery. The London Underground League appealed to his ambition of where he wanted to take the club.

'The reputation and history of the league was what drew us in. There was also the prospect of going up against teams that played more regularly, so our decision was a no-brainer,' explained Fielding.

Fielding had joined the club a year after it was founded, but he had been an employee of South Western Railway FC for far longer, starting his career in September 2011. He had initially joined to get fit and meet new people but before he knew it, he had become the main man behind the team. He had no intentions of taking over when he first joined but that came quickly. Taking over the team didn't affect his playtime as he continued to put his boots on, but the extra responsibility was something he didn't mind taking on.

'I am the organiser, manager, chairman, secretary, treasurer, kit manager and centre-back. In other words, I do everything,' he joked. 'Although I do have a few helping hands when needed or when I am not around.

'The reason for being involved was, at first, for the social and fitness aspect. Being a train driver can get lonely at times and you can often go days or weeks without seeing anyone you are friends with. With the nature of the job being shift work, it can be difficult to keep my fitness and nutritional routine. Joining the team meant meeting new faces and sharing common interests with fellow railway staff. Once the team started to get bigger and we started playing more regular fixtures, I stepped up as an assistant to the original founder, but since he left the company, I took over. He's still a presence, but purely in the background.'

The team had been allocated to Division Two alongside Victoria Line FC, who were set to make their return to the league after their absence. The league wanted to continue following the resumption of grassroots football in 2020 but the postponement of the schedule once again due to the pandemic saw officials opt to promote District Line Railway FC back to the top division and Elizabeth Line FC into Division One in their first season, while adding South Western and the Victoria Line. Fielding was a fan of the two-division split that the league had introduced. He was pleased that the only silverware wasn't a single title at the end of the season, with the divisions allowing for two championship winners on top of the winners in the domestic cups.

'I like it,' he said. 'It keeps the league competitive for all the teams involved as they all have everything to play for. There's the chance to win the league, gain promotion and avoid relegation.'

He wasn't a fan of everything in the league though and he felt very strongly about the team loyalties. He had nothing against the players who decided to play against the line they worked on, but he didn't think it was a good change for the league. His thoughts were simple, and he wondered how it would work with celebrations if a player joined a different team to the line they worked.

'I personally don't like it. It's open to abuse and where does it stop?' Fielding questioned, before continuing, 'You can't say you're a team for Piccadilly, District, Jubilee or even the BTP if some of the players involved aren't your own. You also can't parade a trophy around the workplace of that particular line if the staff of that particular line aren't involved. There's no sense of pride either.'

The rule of playing for your own line was something that Fielding enforced at South Western Railway FC. It wasn't only about pride of playing for the team you worked for and trying to achieve success with your colleagues, but there was no way of encouraging people to join. Fielding had a point too. How would you advertise people to join if you weren't hiring from your own line? The London Underground saw many employees switching between lines due to the nature of the job, something the other teams were well aware of. That was different for South Western, who weren't direct employees of the London Underground network, so there was no chance of having to switch lines and an even smaller chance of having to switch teams.

'We have always maintained that our team would only ever consist of players from South Western Railway. We can't build interest if no one knows anyone involved and can't sustain the future of the team if no one from the place of work knows about it,' said Fielding.

Before they had even made their competitive debut in the league, the club were excited about facing two of the bigger sides in the league, District Line Railway and

Jubilee Line. Their first season wouldn't see them play District Line due to the Stags' promotion, but they could still look forward to a league encounter with Jubilee and the domestic cups could still give them the chance to play District Line. The thought of getting to face these sides was enough to get Fielding buzzing with excitement. He suggested their current rivalries would have stemmed from the friendlies they played before building upon them with competitive action.

'Of course, we will look to create some rivalries. At the moment, that looks to be Jubilee and District Line, purely on having beaten them previously in friendlies. I think there is an element of getting revenge, but I feel all the teams will want to beat us to stamp their authority on the new team,' he joked.

With their debut season coming in 2021/22, Fielding hoped the club could attract new supporters over to Market Road. Although the idea of South Western fans sounded good, he knew that any supporters attending games would be fantastic for coverage and interest in the league.

He said, 'More fans can only be a good thing. More fans bring more social media exposure and that may encourage others in the London Underground to consider starting new or even resurrecting old teams. The league then becomes bigger and better. Maybe more sponsorships and funding then become available to the league.'

Increasing fans also fitted in line with the idea of expanding the league, the idea being that more teams representing different lines would certainly attract more supporters. Those attending games may feel a special bond with certain lines because they live near a station on a particular line or even had a fascination with a line's history. Either way, it would be something to consider.

'I would love to see the league expanded,' said Fielding. 'It can only be a good thing. There are some very good railway football teams out there and to have them on board will only improve the London Underground League whilst gaining more fans and exposure at the same time.'

Football has always been something that Fielding has loved: the emotion, the camaraderie between friends and strangers, as well as getting to be yourself on the pitch. He is also a fan of non-league, regularly attending fixtures. As the chairman of a football team, following the lower leagues gave him inspiration that he could take back to South Western Railway whilst it was a chance to enjoy football as an avid supporter.

'I regularly attend Dulwich Hamlet games, both home and away, so I get to see first hand the brilliant work they do within the local community, schools and the footballing community. I'd say Hamlet inspire me, for sure! They aren't the only club we get our inspiration from,' Fielding said.

'The whole of the non-league community inspires me because despite all the struggles and adversity, they can still have a positive effect in local communities, no matter how big or small [the team]. Without some of these non-league teams, football, and the history of association football as we know it, would be completely different and some of these professional teams wouldn't exist.'

Fielding laughed as he added, 'I'd love to be involved as a player [in non-league] but as a manager – no!'

South Western Railway were still in their infancy when they took the decision to join the London Underground League, being founded just two years prior, but Fielding has huge plans for the club. As long as he was in charge, those ambitions were to go far.

'I would be lying if I don't say to be the best railway [team] in the UK and to be the best team in the London Underground League. Although we want to reach the top, I'd be happy if this team is still in existence when my time on the railway is over.'

8

The Changing Face

SPENCER OWEN and his Hashtag United team filled a tiny dressing room ahead of their first game. The smile grew on the face of each player as they entered the room, seeing their new kits and excited for the journey ahead. The yellow and blue shirts were hung neatly on pegs. Although Hashtag were known as a YouTube team, playing friendlies against other teams who wanted the challenge, the original idea for the club had come about between a few mates.

'It came about really organically. It essentially started as a group of mates coming together for a charity game in memory of one of Spencer's mates. Whilst it was just a kickabout between mates, with Spencer being a content creator, he had an eye on how it might work as content. He started posting highlights online, saw there was an appetite for it and then grew the idea from there and ran with it,' said Hashtag's operations director, Neil Smythe.

As a *FIFA* YouTuber and football content creator, the popular video game was always going to have an influence and inspiration on the plans for Spencer. While it had many different modes, *FIFA Ultimate Team* was the one that he felt would've been the most popular among his viewers.

Smythe said, 'Spencer is very clever as a content creator and thinks very carefully about what will and won't work as a format. He knew there would be a limited appeal and longevity if the early exhibition matches were just posted at random. He knew he had to bring the audience on a journey and added an element of drama to the content. Around the time, there were talks of a "YouTube League", but it would prove too hard to bring all the big YouTubers together to play in a regular structured league. Once that was out of the question, Spencer had to create the idea of a league himself, and being a *FIFA* content creator, the way the game worked was at the forefront of his mind and so the "gamification" of the early chapter was developed.'

Owen opted to use the Divisions mode in *FIFA Ultimate Team* as the idea behind Hashtag United. It was a simple concept that would allow the club to play friendlies but still have something to play for. There was also something to contest for their opponents. Although they had no direct reward, the chance to beat a strong side on camera was another motivation to get people interested. Those who played the computer game knew that this wasn't a normal league format. There were no league tables and the teams only played Hashtag United, and not each other. It was a format suited for a very specific audience.

Smythe said, 'The division format meant the team had to try and achieve a certain number of points in a certain number of games. If they did, they would be rewarded and promoted to the next "division", but if they didn't, they'd stay where they were. This structure built the drama and jeopardy that you wouldn't have had with random friendly games. It also meant their opponents could be organised into categories, with teams playing divisions against the likes of other content creators, staff teams of pro clubs, Sunday league teams and even abroad on mini tours.'

Unlike the video game, where players would begin in Division Ten and try to work their way to the championship of Division One, Hashtag began their journey in Division Five, first going up against other football content creators and real-world companies. Hashtag needed to achieve ten points within ten games to gain promotion to the next division. This was the easiest it would be for Spencer as the divisions would progressively get tougher, requiring more points from the same number of games. They didn't need the full schedule of games though as within four games, Hashtag had picked up a maximum of 12 points, having beaten Dream Team, Copa 90, car manufacturers Vauxhall Motors and the computer game *Football Manager*.

The challenges certainly got harder, with Hashtag needing to use more of their ten games to achieve promotion to the next divisions. The staff teams proved tough opponents in Division Four as they were held by Manchester City staff and lost 2-0 to West Ham United, but despite the difficulties they achieved their target, winning 16 points and only needing 15 for promotion as they were victorious over a range of teams: Umbro, Google and a

Chichester City players celebrate their progress in the FA Cup following their second round tie at Tranmere in December 2019

Prenton Park, 1 December 2019. After holding firm for over an hour, Chichester City eventually lost 5-1 to Tranmere Rovers in the second round of the FA Cup

Dean Cox celebrates his goal during the Sky Bet League One play-off final at Wembley Stadium in May 2014

Jobi McAnuff celebrates with Justin Edinburgh as Leyton Orient win the Vanarama National League at Brisbane Road in April 2019 ...

... and below, he salutes the fans

A dejected Orient fan at the end of the Sky Bet League One play-off final at Wembley Stadium in May 201-

Hashtag United react during the penalty shoot-out loss to Braintree Town during the FA Cup second qualifying round in October 2020

Toby Aromolaran celebrates with team-mates after scoring his side's first goal during the FA Cup second qualifying round in October 2020

Callum Ibe, Dwade James and Steven Carvell all celebrate a goal for Walthamstow against Southend Manor (Andrzej Perkins)

Walthamstow chairman Andy Perkins carried on a stretcher to aid an injured player during the 2021/22 season (Andrzej Perkins)

The Waltham Rabble in full voice as Walthamstow beat Berkhamsted in the FA Cup in September 2021 (Andrzej Perkins)

The Ipswich Town Women players, led by Eloise King, gather to celebrate another victory (Ross Halls)

Friends and family console Ipswich Town Women players following their defeat to Manchester City at the Academy Stadium in February 2020 (Ross Halls)

An Old Spotted Dog poster decorated with the stickers of newly-founded and member-owned Clapton Community (Max Reeves)

Clapton CFC Women pose for a squad photo ahead of their game with Goal Diggers FC (Garry Strutt)

comedians XI (a team including the likes of Omid Djalili, Lloyd Griffiths and Thomas Gray). With Division Four wrapped up, it was on to Division Three where Spencer had accepted challenges from grassroots and non-league teams.

Fox & Hounds, Mongolian Horses and AC Belmont were just a few who took on the Tags, while the club even had a game against Guillem Balagué's Biggleswade United. A defeat to Mongolian Horses and a draw against Freestylers held Hashtag back in their quest but, despite that, they still achieved promotion first time around as they picked up 19 points in eight games. The most notable win was 6-3 over Biggleswade, a semi-pro side playing their football in the Spartan South Midlands League. The victory ultimately wrapped up the division and was a great confidence-booster for the side.

The confidence was needed if they were to keep their streak of winning each division at their first attempt and Division Two was their toughest to date. The schedule included facing several Sunday league clubs and fellow YouTube sides as well as a star-studded team. Hashtag picked up maximum points from their first five games of Division Two, beating Palmers FC, JD Club NI, Soccer AM, Eltham SF, and Coke United. Although they had made a great start, the winning run was brought to an end by Atlanta United staff. Hashtag had a brief return to winning ways as they defeated the staff of New York City, but wins for Warmballers FC and Star Sixes (a team including Robert Pires and Emile Heskey) left Hashtag needing a win in their final game to secure promotion to

Division One. The end of the season was the drama the club had wanted to create for their audience. They had won all the divisions they played first time around but to keep that up, they had to beat their sponsors, Top Eleven.

The game resulted in a 6-0 thrashing of the staff at Top Eleven, securing Hashtag's passage to the top division as they looked to round the series off in style. They needed 22 points from the ten games available to secure the title they had set out to win from the beginning. The division was tight and with seven wins, one draw and two losses, Hashtag scrapped to the title by the thinnest of margins. Crystal Palace staff, Arsenal for Everyone, the GB Deaf Team, Aston Villa staff, St John's FC, Stoke City and Pitchero United were no match for the YouTube elites, but Football Fancast and Arsenal Fan TV were certainly up for the task, while non-league Beaconsfield Town managed to hold them to a draw as each side looked to derail their title hopes.

Spencer had also led his team out at Wembley Stadium several times. The 2015 and 2016 editions of the Wembley Cup saw his original team, Spencer FC, feature against Sidemen United (a team created by YouTube's Sidemen) and Weller Wanderers, a team captained by YouTuber Joe Weller, claiming both titles before Hashtag took over. The Tags' first match at Wembley saw them beat Tekkers Town, a team captained by the F2 Freestylers, 6-1 in 2017, before the following year saw a change in format of the competition. Instead of just a final, Spencer had introduced a format that saw four teams competing for the ultimate prize. Each side would play each of the others in a group-stage game before there would be semi-finals followed by the final. Hashtag had got off to the best possible start in the group stage as they beat Rebel FC before going on to beat XO FC and F2 FC. The three wins from three saw them finish top of their group while all the other sides had won just one of their three games. Their hopes of another Wembley Cup title were cut short in the semi-final as they were beaten by Rebel FC with Jesse Waller Lassen scoring the only goal of the game. With Hashtag out of the running, the eventual winners were F2, with over 34,000 people in attendance.

'I wasn't there but I knew how all the guys felt,' explained Smythe. 'Every football supporter dreams of going to Wembley as a fan. But how many get to play there alongside some of their heroes?'

The Wembley Cup hadn't just involved YouTubers keen to play at the Home of Football – plenty of legends also got involved. Jamie Carragher, Robert Pires, Patrick Kluivert, Peter Schmeichel and Jay-Jay Okocha were some of the big names getting their boots on again.

Smythe said, 'The lucky ones played in front of 34,000 and if you ask anyone that played, they will say the Wembley Cup was some of the best days of their life. We now work with players who have been in the non-league game for years and have never got to play there, including our manager Jay Devereux. Giving them the chance to play and manage there, albeit a friendly, was incredible.'

Ahead of the 2018/19 season, Spencer had made the decision to take Hashtag United to the next level. They were well known as a YouTube team but he and the club wanted more than that. They wanted the prospect of competing for league titles and cups to become a reality.

Smythe explained, 'Spencer always thinks several steps ahead. There was probably going to be a time limit on the lifespan of the first chapter of the club; it's always going to be hard to keep the narrative going if you're always playing friendly games, and we've seen some YouTube teams disband for that reason. We needed to move the club on and taking the leap into non-league was the obvious step, once we knew that there were slots available. Spencer had an interest in local non-league football for a while, and even made a series about East Thurrock years ago, which was where he met Devs [Devereux], who was John Coventry's assistant.'

Hashtag took the biggest leap into their next chapter in 2018 as they exercised their plans to join the pyramid. They joined the National League System at Step 6, nine levels below the Premier League, and were assigned to the Spartan South Midlands League. With the majority of the squad based in Essex, the league didn't suit their needs and as a result Hashtag contested their placement.

'There was never an indication that we would be put in the Spartan League until it was announced suddenly. It came as a shock,' said Smythe. 'We would have struggled to play in the league because it would have meant the players travelling further which would have either cost them or the club; moving leagues is a problem many non-league clubs struggle with. The biggest problem was that going into the Spartan League meant taking the place of an existing team and we simply wouldn't have done that. The Eastern Counties League needed more teams, and we weren't taking anyone's place by entering that league.'

Their first season had seen them take the non-league world by storm, winning promotion from Eastern Counties Division One South against all the odds. No one had expected the start the club had made. Losses against Little Oakley and White Ensign and draws against Hackney Wick and Wivenhoe Town meant Hashtag won only two points in their first four games and had given them a difficult start to the season. They recorded their first win at Step 6 against Braintree Town Reserves, kicking off an incredible run towards the title.

They had gone on a 14-game unbeaten run between August and early December, winning 13 and drawing one before they faced a defeat against Harwich & Parkeston. That defeat, only their third of the season, reminded Hashtag just how difficult non-league was regardless of their good form. The mentality of the group had begun to shine through as they picked up more momentum and form. The loss to Harwich had kick-started a brief period of form, going four games unbeaten with wins against Newbury Forest, Brightlingsea Regent Reserves and Fire United and drawing with Benfleet. That run was ended by Wormley Rovers but that didn't hold Hashtag back as they recorded ten wins and two draws in their final 12 games and marched to promotion.

Smythe said, 'It was certainly unexpected given the start we made. I think we were five games in before we won a game. If you had asked any one of us, having not won a single game and knowing there was only one guaranteed spot, we would probably have said that promotion was unlikely. Once we found the winning mentality, I think everyone at the club knew something special was building.

'By Christmas, we had gone on a run of 11 wins in a row. We knew there was the possibility [of going up], but we had still given ourselves so much to do. We knew we probably had to win every one of our remaining games and, despite losing one in January, we won every single game until the title was won. As the cliché goes, every game was a cup final, and we just had to focus on the game in front of us and not worry about the other teams in the hunt. While we were winning our games, our title rivals were picking each other off one by one and dropping points. By the end of the season, we had such an incredible save made by Jamie 'Jacko' Jackson, in particular against Wormley and Halstead, which was key in that run. We finally pulled it off at one of the most historic grounds in London, the Old Spotted Dog, which made it even more special.'

Hashtag's season in the Eastern Counties League was never going to be easy. It would have been difficult for them to build profiles on their opponents and the standard of non-league football generally, having only had experience playing Sunday league and friendlies, even if a couple of the wins came against non-league sides. That was not made any easier by the start they had made to the 2018/19 season.

Smythe continued, 'As I said, it was tough because of the start we had made. And we gave teams a head start. You don't expect teams to have to go on two runs of ten wins in a row to win a league. It was tough but the big difference between the league last year and this season [2019/20], was there were teams last season that you'd expect to beat. The manager would never say this but there were teams who were noticeably easier to play against than others, so when we were on a difficult run, to a certain extent, you could see an easier game ahead. There were no points in the Essex Senior League where anyone thought that. The strength in depth in the ESL is much stronger than the Eastern Counties League.'

Following their promotion, Hashtag had been assigned to the Essex Senior League. It was always going to be a tougher competition but it was a great reward for their previous season's work. The league was full of teams who sought promotion and had come remarkably close previously. Enfield had finished third in 2013/14 behind Haringey Borough and Great Wakering Rovers but had missed out on promotion by two points, while Clapton had fallen eight points short of promotion as Barking had accumulated 100 points to their 92 in 2016/17. Stansted had missed out most recently by just five points as Hullbridge Sports won the title in 2018/19 with 87 points.

'It was very tough,' recalled Smythe. 'We lost our first game of the season to Southend Manor which gave us a wake-up call. We never took anyone lightly but to lose that first game was a real blow.'

That defeat wasn't the only thing that made the season tough, as Hashtag had suffered several injuries which left them needing to bring in a few reinforcements to shore up the squad.

Smythe said, 'What really made the season tougher was the injury list that Devs had to deal with. By the end of 2019, our midfield and defence in particular were decimated. From the team that had won the league last year, we lost Jacko in pre-season as well as our captain Jack Harrison. We then lost Tom Williams, Ross Gleed and Ricky Evans, so we were really at bare bones and had lost a few leaders. We had to bring in a fair number of players and it's huge credit to those who joined because they fitted in so well and helped us out when we needed it. We probably overachieved given the issues we'd had with injuries. With opponents, the big difference between the two seasons was there were no gimmes and this shows when you look at the teams that beat us. After we lost to Southend Manor, we had also lost to Sporting Bengal United, two talented teams who weren't fighting at the top. We had a real scare against Woodford Town, and then at the top, we had some titanic clashes with Walthamstow, Hadley, and Saffron Walden Town. It would have been an interesting run-in.'

The 2019/20 season was only Hashtag's second in non-league, but they soon found themselves battling for another title. The opening-day loss was put to the back of their minds as they went on a ten-game winning run, starting with a 6-0 victory over Tower Hamlets. Devereux had really pushed his side towards a second promotion. Defeats to Sporting Bengal and Hadley either side of a four-game winning streak seemed to be minor blips in their progress as seven wins and two draws between December and March, including a huge victory against Walthamstow, kept them on track. That put them in pole position for the title, but they never got to finish the season. There was no doubt that the Hashtag players and management were confident in their ability to win the league and gain promotion.

Smythe said, 'We always believed. We had always believed from the previous season because as a sportsman, you have to believe otherwise you have already lost. Did anyone think it was won? Absolutely not! We had a quarter of the season left to play and we had some really tough games ahead of us. Saffron Walden were always going to be up against it when you look at the games in hand us and Walthamstow had.

'We would have had to go there on the final day and whether it would have been sewn up by then, I don't know. The really important games in the race were the ones just before the season was voided; Saffron Walden at home could have gone either way, we ground out a result against Hadley which was really key because we put an end to their hopes, and then we had the games against Walthamstow which were so tight. The away leg was won by a breakaway goal and the home leg could have gone either way on a pitch that was an absolute lottery. We were very aware of that. The title race wasn't over but we had put ourselves in a really good position, and what was different from the previous season was our points-per-game was looking really strong so the likelihood was that two teams would have gone up.'

Due to decisions out of their control, the 2019/20 season being voided meant Hashtag would still be playing in the Essex Senior League for 2020/21. They had to prepare for a far tougher season than they had experienced previously as teams hoped to pip them to the top spot. No one had anticipated another halted campaign, so Hashtag had to remain focused on the task in hand when the season finally came around.

Smythe explained, 'It's easy to look back on that with hindsight, knowing that the two voided seasons would come down to points-per-game. When you look back, every game was important in getting us promoted. Going into last season, we had the mindset that we needed to start with a fresh slate and put the disappointment of the voided season behind us.

'We expected as close to a full season as possible, and I certainly don't think we expected a quarter of the season to be played and that be it. It was about going into the season with a positive mindset, and I've got to say, I have an awful lot of respect for Devs and the team for turning it around and pulling it off.'

Before they could get their Essex Senior League campaign under way, Hashtag made their bow in the FA Cup, entering at the extra preliminary round stage. It had been an unusual way to start the season as teams had often played two or three games by the time the annual competition got going. Hashtag's debut was already going to be a memorable and nervy affair, but it was made much tougher as their opening game of 2020/21.

Smythe said, 'It was hard because no one wants to go into such an important game that early in the season, but every game was important. For us, it was big. It was our debut in the FA Cup and that first game meant so much to Spencer, his family and Devs as well, as he led the guys into the battle in that first campaign. We worked hard in pre-season, and like most teams, you can't tell too much from pre-season, but we had started really slowly. We were on the back of a thrashing from Welling Town quite early in pre-season and, from then, the pressure was on. Our pre-season picked up against sides higher than us in the pyramid, with results against Great Wakering Rovers and Grays Athletic, and from that you could see the guys were ready. You never wanted to start the season with such an important game, but that was our toughest test in the cup.'

Hashtag didn't let that affect them and continued to look towards the future. The 2019 Women's World Cup had inspired chairman Spencer Owen to get involved with women's football. The initial idea was to sponsor a women's side, helping them to develop on and off the pitch. The plan soon changed when he realised he could form a team of his own that would come under the Hashtag umbrella, Hashtag United Women.

Smythe said, 'There was a lot of work [to form a women's team]. People questioned why we didn't have one earlier in our history, but it was a simple case of needing to walk before we could run. We were already entering a world that was alien to some of us and we simply couldn't do everything at once. When you don't have a home, every team you add increases the cost and makes it really hard to get other teams off the ground.

'Spencer got inspired by the Women's World Cup and he vowed to support a women's side last summer. His original plan was to sponsor one, but then he realised he could do something more substantial and when he was thinking of bringing women's football to the club, it was a question of would we start from scratch or would we merge with another team. A few clubs approached him, but the fit didn't seem right. When AFC Basildon came to talk to him, it was a great match. The club had a history and a pedigree but had faced struggles over the years so we could hopefully give them the stability they needed to push on. Ultimately, they also wanted to be part of what we were doing, and we were excited to be part of women's football. We couldn't wait to get started together.'

Hashtag had also looked towards their youth development as a future venture for the club. On top of entering a reserve side into the Essex Senior League Reserve Division ahead of the 2020/21 season, they had also merged with Forest Glade, giving children the chance to play under the Hashtag banner.

'Youth development should be on the roadmap of any club that wants to grow and give something back to the local community and the next generation of players. It hasn't happened for us in the traditional way as of yet because we had to find our feet in non-league first, but both our mergers with AFC Basildon and Forest Glade FC now give us the foundation to develop youth players, both boys and girls,' said Smythe.

In 2017, when Hashtag were still just a YouTube team, Spencer had introduced an academy series in which just under 20,000 applications had been sent with players looking to join. They had been boiled down to a select number of lucky applicants and those who were chosen faced the tests in front of Spencer and other Hashtag players. After various challenges and 18 players being cut down to just two finalists, Scott Pollock and Jack Durkin, 16-year-old Pollock was announced as the winner, signing for Hashtag United on a one-year contract and picking up £3,000 in the process.

Smythe said, 'The academy was certainly an original way for us to help develop some young players whilst offering an audience an aspirational opportunity, the chance to be part of the team. Seb [Spencer's brother] famously spotted Scott as one to watch very early on in that first series but very few would have predicted how his career has progressed since winning it. He went from playing for us, and being man of the match at Wembley, to securing a pro contract at Northampton Town, and we're so proud of him. Scott wasn't actually the only decent player they found in the first series. Others went on to become vital players of the club and some have since been knocking on the door at pro clubs.'

Hashtag needed to find a home but where would a team with just an online presence be based? For Spencer, that was Essex. Until they had their own ground, in the distant future, the club had to ground-share wherever was available and since their inception in the National League System, the Tags have called three places home: Coles Park, Chadfields and the Len Salmon Stadium. Having begun in north London, they soon moved towards the sea to Chadfields, the home of Tilbury FC, before going a few stops further down the line ahead of the 2020/21 season. They certainly hadn't planned to have that many homes but factors that affected the future of the club meant a constant move across the last three seasons. They hoped to have settled at the home of Bowers & Pitsea for now, with the chance to build upon their newfound home.

Smythe said, 'The roots of the club are Essex. It's where Spencer is from, and he sees the club as an Essex club. It's way too early to be talking about building our own ground. It's not as easy as that. We want to lay our roots in Essex and it's unfortunate we have had three grounds already. We had to leave Coles Park [the home of Haringey Borough] because towards the end of the 2018/19 season, we had been given an indication that there was a possible restructure of league borders coming and because the ground was towards the northern end of the area, there was a chance we would have been put in the Spartan [South Midlands League], although it didn't pan out that way in the end. A move of 20 or 30 miles away can really shift the cost base and the fan base of non-league teams and there are clubs that have almost folded because they have been moved into a sideways league.

'Haringey Borough and Tilbury were great landlords. Tilbury bent over backwards for us as they built Spencer a lovely commentary booth, let us put in super-fast broadband and even painted a hashtag on the wall. They were amazing but we had to think about the future potential of the club and there was an opportunity at Bowers to not only run our home games, but to also train – we had struggled finding somewhere to train – and the real catalyst for the move was the potential to host our BTEC education programme. Sadly, that couldn't happen for another year due to the current climate, but obviously, the move had happened, and we are looking forward to building with Bowers & Pitsea.'

9

Counting Clean Sheets

JAMES BRANSGROVE didn't always want to be a footballer. As a young kid his ambitions had been elsewhere, but he knew from early on that it would be tough. Football for him was a second choice but it was a career path that took him towards his goal of being a professional athlete. Like every child who dreamt of one day playing for a professional team, he would find himself running around a playground, kicking a football with ambitions of reaching the highest level he could, but when he put the gloves on and found himself between the sticks, he didn't expect to reach such heights.

'I didn't take it overly serious, I must admit. Looking back at it, I think I took my lunchtime playground football more serious than my actual football,' he said. 'I had always wanted to be a professional cricketer but realistically, I was never good enough. Although, I did find myself in and around breaking into the Essex youth teams.'

Bransgrove found himself in the academies of professional clubs from a young age as he sought to become an athlete. After signing for Leyton Orient, he spent several years in east London as he crafted his trade. It wasn't quite what he imagined and he soon found himself moving on from the O's. Once he had done that, he was soon journeying with his school friends through various local teams before being signed to Buckhurst Hill. He wanted to just play football, but the expectations of a young player were beyond what he was cut out for.

'I was fortunate enough to be signed for Leyton Orient at a young age. I was picked up at the age of six or seven and stayed at the club until I was 12 when I decided to leave. I didn't enjoy training three times a week at such a young age. I played with school-mates at various local teams for a few years, spending the majority of the time outfield, before [aged] 16 onwards, I went back in goal. I recall one season where I played the first half in goal and then the second half up front, scoring 26 goals in the process. I wouldn't necessarily say I took it overly serious, but I was fortunate enough to be part of a successful Buckhurst Hill side – I believe six of us went on to turn professional.'

A year later, a teenage Bransgrove signed for another top club. This time, it was a move across London as Brentford acquired his signature. It hadn't been a straightforward switch from Buckhurst Hill over to the Bees but after a string of superb performances on the pitch, the move slowly gathered momentum.

'My footballing between the ages of 16 and 17 was a bit of a blur – it's unthinkable what happened! After being part of a successful Buckhurst Hill side, I was forwarded on to Tottenham Hotspur for a trial where I trained for six weeks. I was told they couldn't sign me because I looked too baby-faced, and I lacked an imposing presence. I remember going home after that and crying. After that rejection, a schoolfriend's dad was the manager of Waltham Abbey under-18s and asked me if I wanted to help them out for one game as their usual keeper was injured. I played – away to Colchester – and had a blinder. The next day, I had received a call from the reserves manager who asked me to play for them on a Saturday. Again, I had a blinder.

'What happened the next day? I got a phone call from the first-team manager, Paul Wickenden. After our chat, I was called up to the first team as the number two, owing so much to him and his dad, Ray. When their first-choice keeper was injured, I was chucked in. Six or seven games later, I was off to Brentford.'

For James, it was certainly a unique experience. He was studying for his A-Levels so Brentford allowed him to stay at sixth form for his exams, and he only trained twice a week. It was the highest level he had played but after doing well at youth level, the next step of under-21 football level was a real struggle for him.

'Brentford offered me the chance to return the following pre-season to earn a professional contract as they were unsure about me. I rejected the offer because they wouldn't offer me digs during the pre-season period, meaning a four-hour round commute on the Underground every day. I felt it was very elitist and undermining for young players.'

With the move to Brentford off the table in the summer, it wasn't long before he was on the radar of another professional football club.

'Colchester United were aware of me, my unique background and that I'd left Brentford. I had an agent at the time so within two days of leaving, I was on a two-week trial with Colchester. I settled in immediately and I had an amazing first day's trial. I was glad that I knew they'd sign me after the first day.'

Bransgrove was successful with Colchester's under-18s, winning the Football League Youth South East and Football League Alliance Cup in 2013/14.

'Colchester was meant to be. They understood my circumstances and appreciated I had had a bit of an astronomical rise, so they were unbelievably accommodating. They let me spend my first year as a pro within the youth teams as an over-aged player – being a keeper, this was allowed. There was no special treatment for me; I trained with the youth, playing with them and had all the usual jobs like boot cleaning. It made sense to join them.

'In truth, it was a season of highs and lows. I started off phenomenally, and by October I was awarded a professional contract for the following season. From about November to February, I really struggled. Looking back now, I feel I was simply burnt out. My body wasn't used to the full-time demands and, unlike how I am today, I wasn't fit enough. I feel I had pushed myself too much too soon but at the time, it was hard to see that. I ended the season in good form, which was the cherry on top. I was lucky enough to have almost every game and contribute significantly, which is always a bonus. We won the league on the final day, in the final minute, against Wimbledon before going on to win the national cup against Bradford in their own back yard at Valley Parade in front of 5,000 spectators, which was superb. It was reassurance to myself that I could compete at the top level and my decision to join Colchester was the right one.'

While playing for Colchester, Bransgrove had also made his Scotland debut with the under-18s. He had qualified to play for the Scots as his mother was from Glasgow but accidentally found out about his call-up when he was about to play a game.

'This was another piece to the rollercoaster journey, I must say,' he added jokingly. 'We had a youth game at home to Stevenage and one my under-16 coaches came up to me before kick-off and congratulated me on my Scotland call-up. I looked at him rather confused before he apologised, told me to forget it and ran off. I spent the whole game thinking about it, trying to work out what he was talking about.

'After the game, the head of youth – Tony Humes – called me into his office and explained that I had been invited to a Scotland under-18s training camp for three days. I can only imagine it came from our impressive start to the season. I believe we had won ten and drawn two after 12 games. This was another great experience. Some fantastic players were there, many of whom you'd watch on your TV in the Premier League and SPL today, but that was another indication to myself that I could compete at the highest level.'

For any player, being called up to the first team was a special moment. Bransgrove achieved that very feat in 2014 when he was named in Colchester's squad for their FA Cup first-round tie away to Gosport Borough. It wasn't a simple call though and he hadn't prepared to make the trip on the Sunday morning. Although he was an unused substitute in the U's 6-3 win over Gosport, it was still a proud moment for the keeper.

'I was originally on standby for our number-two keeper, Chris Lewington, as his wife was due to give birth any day,' Bransgrove explained. 'I was told on the Friday to keep my phone on all day and, if required, I would have to drive down to Gosport if Chris had to drive home. I heard nothing by late Saturday night, so I turned my phone off. The only reason I turned it back on the next morning was because it was Remembrance Sunday and my mum had dragged me out of bed.

'Ten minutes later, I got the call to travel down to Gosport. I have my mum to thank for waking me, as if she hadn't, I would have been in big trouble.

'It was an amazing experience. I got my first shirt – Bransgrove, 29 – so I'd finally achieved something I never thought I would as a kid. To make it even better, as it was Remembrance Sunday, it was a special kit with a poppy sewn on it, so we got to keep it. The shirt is still hanging in my room today.'

For Bransgrove, it seemed like everything was coming up trumps. That was until 2015 when he suffered his first serious injury, a real setback for a player who was doing so well. The injury was tough to take and with everything going so well for Bransgrove, it seemed to have all come crashing back to earth. Footballers have regularly struggled both physically and mentally following a serious injury, and it was no different for Bransgrove.

'The injury was tough to take, and I struggled. This was the biggest impact on my career after I had had a fantastic season and was close to being made second-choice keeper at the age of 19. I had also enjoyed a fantastic loan spell with Bishop's Stortford in the Conference South and everything I seemed to do turned to gold. I had started to push myself on and off the field so it may have been me, making my own fortune. Sadly, on the penultimate day of the season, I felt my knee give way in the warm-up and I was ruled out for nine months with a flipped and torn meniscus.

'I remember the moment I was told I would be out for months. I hobbled out of the doctor's room and cried. I cried because, for one, everything I worked hard for was now gone, and secondly, I would have also had a summer of cricket. It was just so tough mentally.'

Bransgrove had several loan spells while he was signed to Colchester, returning to non-league football. He was still a young and hungry player so loans in tough leagues further down the pyramid were a good step.

'My first loan at [Bishop's] Stortford was great. I learnt a lot there and playing under Rob Stringer as a 19-year-old was a real experience, especially in the midst of a relegation battle. It certainly manned me up and improved my game. I had another loan at Maldon & Tiptree which allowed me to get fit after my injury and again that was great. I got to play in a league I was familiar with and, although it was lower to what I had played previously, it was a great confidence booster.

'My third loan was to Wealdstone, again in the Conference South, but that loan was pretty rubbish to be honest. It felt rushed and manufactured. The move came about because the goalkeeper coach knew their coach, so it was sorted in a few hours. I was cover for their keeper for a month as he was out with an injury. I have nothing against the club as I've met some great people who I am still in touch with today, but deep down, I don't think I was really wanted – maybe that's just me! I started off well but then I had an okay game against Sutton and a pretty poor game against Oxford and that was that.'

Following the loans away from Colchester, Bransgrove finally made his professional debut for the club in May 2016. He wasn't in the best condition as he had struggled to recover from his injury and felt he was stuck in a single gear when it came to his performance. To make matters worse, he had picked up another injury in training before the game but that was the least of his concerns as he lined up against Rochdale in League One. The misfortune of keeper Dillion Barnes meant he was thrown in at the last minute and Barnes missed the opportunity for his very own debut.

Bransgrove said, 'I was personally stuck in fourth gear performance wise as I struggled to get over my injury. Two days before the final game of the season, I dislocated my finger in training and it got to the point where I wanted the season to be over with. I'd had enough. I wasn't in the matchday squad for the final game of the season so I could have easily gone out with mates or had a late night, but I still remember having an early night.

'There had been an accident on the A12, and it was shut for hours. Sadly, Dillion hadn't seen this and was stuck in it. Coincidentally, he had dropped his phone and broke it that day – so nobody actually knew where he was! We had no fit goalkeeper at the club; the number-one keeper had a back injury so all of a sudden, at 2.15pm when Dillion hadn't arrived, I was in. I had a shirt printed, had my fingers strapped up and several painkillers shoved down my throat, with the lightest of warm-ups 30 minutes before kick-off. Not a lot went through my head as there was no time to really think about it. It was so rushed and unscripted. You couldn't make it up. What made it easier was we had already been relegated and Rochdale were mid-table with nothing to play for.'

It had been a tough season for Colchester. After winning just nine of their 46 games, they finished 23rd and ten points from safety. The final game ended in defeat for Bransgrove and the U's. Nathaniel Mendez-Laing had broken the deadlock for Rochdale in the 18th minute but an equaliser from Joe Edwards wasn't enough for a point as Calvin Andrew netted the winner for Dale.

Despite only making his professional debut a few months prior, in December 2016, Bransgrove brought his career to an end. A promising start to life as a Colchester player did not continue that way and his decision to retire at a young age was one that was well thought.

'It's something that had been on my mind for a year or so,' he explained. 'I struggled to recover from my knee injury, which was a big factor, and looking up at the scoreboard on my debut and thinking "Only 15 minutes left, thank God!" was another factor. The final nail in the coffin, amongst many other things, was my final game for the under-23s. I had an awful game, because I didn't want to be there, and I chucked the fifth one in, walked off the pitch and didn't care the least. That was the tell-tale sign for me as I've always prided myself on my professionalism and giving my best for my team, team-mates and myself.'

After a spell away from football completely, Bransgrove returned to play whilst studying for a business degree. His time playing professionally was over but that didn't stop him wanting to return to non-league. From his early retirement, he signed for Chelmsford City in the National League South before dropping down the pyramid to play for Coggeshall Town at Step 5 of the National League System.

He said, 'Chelmsford was just an emergency backup spell. I knew the manager, Rob Stringer, from my Stortford loan and he asked if I would help out if their only keeper got injured as the transfer window was closed and they were going into the play-offs. I never trained with them or went to a game.

'I took almost a year out. I was lucky to have many offers but I turned them down as I really had no ambitions to play. In September 2017, I had a phone call from Coggeshall Town. I mutually knew the assistant manager and some of my old Colchester United youth and under-23 team-mates played for them. The ground was also close to where I worked so I decided to give it a go. We had a great team, and I had a great time, not looking back since.'

Coggeshall won the Eastern Counties League Premier Division in 2017/18, collecting a massive 115 points and scoring 145 goals. They finished six points above second-placed Felixstowe & Walton United. It was such a great achievement and the photo of the title-winning squad sits proudly on the club's website for all to see.

After his departure from the Seed Growers, Bransgrove joined Walthamstow in the Essex Senior League, going across Step 5 to another league.

'Unfortunately, I fell out with the manager at Coggeshall after I felt he disrespected me. Again, I was fortunate to have several offers, but I chose Walthamstow as it's close to my home and the manager, Ryan Maxwell, was comfortable with me not committing to training full-time – mainly because I had two big accounting exams in March. My old Coggeshall team-mate, Correy Davidson, was the agent behind this and was the one who made Maxy aware of who I was.'

In east London, Bransgrove certainly enjoyed his football. He started in all 20 games he played for Stow and helped them to a third-placed finish in 2018/19. He came into the squad against Saffron Walden Town, managing to help the Blues on to a 3-1 win over the Bloods. It only took three games before he kept his first clean sheet and he then clocked up another ten towards the end of the season.

The following season, Bransgrove became the go-to keeper for Walthamstow as he made a further 34 appearances, starting in 33 as a keeper and coming on as a sub against Tower Hamlets, playing up front and getting a goal in the Errington Challenge Cup, a domestic cup competition for the Essex Senior League teams. Despite being marked by two defenders, he managed to use his height to rise above them and head beyond his usual opposition number. The celebrations for the goal were wild as neither team-mates nor fans could believe what they had seen. But, although Bransgrove started 2019/20 for Walthamstow, due to factors beyond his control he decided to leave. With manager Ryan Maxwell departing and with rumours flying around, he felt he couldn't be part of the team.

'It was tough, very tough [to leave]. We as a team had achieved so much in a short space of time and I'd made some great friends. It's a cliché to say, especially in non-league, but the politics behind it all didn't sit well with me and I didn't want to associate myself with all the rumours that had been going around with regards to the departure of Maxy and how the club was run,' Bransgrove said.

His next move had seen him head up the leagues to the Isthmian League Premier Division with Bowers & Pitsea in search of a long-term option. Leaving Walthamstow meant he hadn't trained or played so when he climbed the pyramid, he knew he needed to get his fitness back before he could be in contention for the squad. He expected his time at the new club to go well but towards the end of 2019/20, the halt in the season meant his plans had changed.

'Bowers & Pitsea was meant to be a long-term signing. I had nearly signed for them before I signed for Walthamstow and after some time in the lower leagues, I felt like pushing myself up again. The manager, Rob Small, asked me to come in and was happy with my request to have four weeks or so to get fit – I hadn't had much goalkeeper training so to immediately step into Isthmian League football wouldn't have been fair on myself, in my opinion.

'I got fit and was due to play Kingstonian but, sadly, COVID came along and ruined it all. In the summer, I accepted an offer from Bowers to stay and be number one, which I was excited for. Again, due to the virus, my university commitments changed and, going into my sixth and final year, I could no longer commit to the demands of Step 3 football. Bowers announced my departure and Dunmow Town asked me to be part of their project. I knew those behind the scenes, which made it an easy choice, and also the lower standard meant I could have nights off training to study – that worked perfectly. As before, at the time, it just made sense.'

Dunmow Town had been founded ahead of the 2020/21 season by Simon Noakes, a businessman with a dream of owning a club. Their first season would see them playing in the Essex and Suffolk Border League, Step 7, which meant Bransgrove had dropped further down the non-league ladder in order to play. Arguably, he was far better than the level suggested, but playing there meant he was also able to study, which was his main focus. He didn't want to let his studies prevent him from playing but he also didn't want his football to affect his studying. But, after playing just a few games at the start of the new season, Bransgrove departed and sought a new challenge.

'I moved on from Dunmow simply because I felt they didn't need me. We won games seven- and eight-nil and in one of the games, I didn't touch the ball and had a sunbathe. I did apologise to the other team afterwards as I know that's rather disrespectful. Again, I was in a fortunate position to receive several offers, but the Essex Senior League appealed to me as it was a standard that could still accommodate my university work and studying requirements.'

His career path had taken him back to Step 5 and the Essex Senior League, the very league he had left towards the end of the 2019/20 season. Saffron Walden Town were looking to build a strong squad that would help compete for the title like they had done during the season that Bransgrove had played for Stow. The move also meant he would face his former side and would again meet the Waltham Rabble standing behind his goal, trying to put him off. It was going to be his first experience of being on the other end of their banter. On Saturday, 24 October 2020, the clubs met at Saffron Walden's Catons Lane ground in the ESL. It was a tight game that both sides had hoped to win but a penalty from Dwade James was enough for Walthamstow to claim the three points.

'It was weird but at the same time enjoyable,' Bransgrove said about being on the opposing side. 'I thought they'd give me more stick, but I would like to think I'm a good guy and, whoever I represent, I give my best for. If I ever come up against an old team, I'd like to think they remember that and respect that.'

His theory worked as both parties showed a mutual respect for each other. While they were rivals on the pitch, both had shared good times over the past few seasons.

Away from football, Bransgrove's focus was on passing his degree and working towards a career. He wasn't sure if he would continue to play once his studies were over, but he hoped he wouldn't have to give it up. Sadly, only time would tell.

'After graduation, my aim is to then complete my ACCA exams to become fully chartered before possibly taking a master's in finance. Who knows where I will be? Four years ago, I was a professional footballer so let's see what the next four bring,' said Bransgrove.

'I'm hoping my studies and qualifications open a few more avenues for me with regards to my career prospects. I have always said my career comes first so if I have to choose between working more and playing football, I will choose my career, sadly.'

10

Community

CLAPTON ARE one of the oldest clubs in London, having been founded over 140 years ago in 1877 and with a strong following. Based in Hackney Downs and fewer than five miles from London Docklands, Clapton were all about community and served it throughout generations of players and fans. They were an unloved club fighting at the bottom of the table, but while the supporters had returned and Clapton had found a new spark, a long era of serving the community had ended following a takeover.

The takeover saw the dismantling of the membership and the club had become isolated from the community, falling to its lowest point. Supporters and volunteers were unsuccessful in getting Clapton to open to the community after years of trying to do so, putting the future of the club and London's oldest senior football ground in serious peril. Supporters and members for life took decisive action to keep the legacy of Clapton alive and, in 2018, Clapton Community was voted into existence.

'We pulled away from Clapton FC due to the intransigence and hostility of the chief executive, who did not want to engage with or open up the club membership to us. This was despite the fact that within the space of a couple of years, Clapton's average gate had risen from 20 to nearly 300. The toxic relationship led to the lengthy boycott of home games, hoping that such a move and lost revenue would lead to the more enlightened attitude of the club. The growing frustration and futility of standing outside the Old Spotted Dog on a Saturday afternoon eventually led us in a more positive direction, thus Clapton CFC was born,' said committee member Gary Price.

The creation of the new club meant that Clapton CFC fans weren't planning on going back to the Essex Senior League anytime soon to support the original Clapton.

'The straightforward answer is no,' said Joe Cassidy, when asked whether he and other Clapton fans would switch back. 'Clapton CFC is my club now, in a way the other Clapton never was. I am co-owner, shareholder and committee member; roles that were never open to me at the other club. "Support the team, not the regime" was a popular slogan during the fans' time at the Old Spotted Dog and we supported the team passionately home and away. Frustration grew at the way the club was being run and the CEO's lack of transparency and refusal to engage with us.

This ultimately led to the formation of Clapton CFC. Presently, the other Clapton have no home and little support and they increasingly bear little relation to the other club.

We see ourselves as the inheritors of the Clapton history and legacy, a belief that is gaining momentum in the wider footballing world.'

The name of the club gives the impression it does exactly what it says on the tin. Clapton Community FC wants to be at the forefront and be open to anyone who wants to support them in a respectful way. It isn't just about football either; the club does everything they can to support the local community.

Price said, 'Clapton Community above all stands for community. The message we send out is one of inclusiveness, that people irrespective of background or race can watch football in a safe and welcoming environment. A sign at our home games says "no dickheads". We are very proactive in supporting worthwhile causes and there is a food bank collection at every home game.'

While CCFC wanted to welcome as many new fans as they could, they wanted to ensure it stayed welcome. That didn't necessarily mean they wanted to control their supporters; how could they ensure everyone followed the rules if hundreds attended each game? They couldn't, but they had a way around that.

Price explained, 'All members of the club sign up to an accountability agreement which means that they agree to our ethos and are accountable for their actions. This is the beginning point we hope will start conversations in the community that we are building about what it means to be anti-racist, anti-fascist and anti-sexist. Of course, we can't control everyone who comes to watch the games. It's a more succinct approach. Fans can support the team however they wish, just don't be a dickhead!'

That message was passed on to fans and the wider community through the way the club engaged with those people. They always wanted to learn lessons from what they had experienced at Clapton FC to ensure they didn't make the same mistakes which led to a demise in crowd sizes and support.

'Our fanbase has naturally grown through being inclusive and keeping members and fans engaged in the decision-making of the club, but also by being welcoming and a fun place to come every matchday. Our fanbase comes from the local communities, the football community and our international community,' said Price.

Price had been captivated by several clubs in the Isthmian League – Dulwich Hamlet, Corinthian Casuals and Wycombe Wanderers in the 1960s – but Clapton held an advantage for his affection. A club from east London, it was only a mile away from his first love, West Ham United. At the same time, he was looking for another footballing home as the corporate and commercialised world that the Hammers had come to represent wasn't for him.

Despite the poor results of Clapton, he fell in love with the club after making his first and subsequent visits to the Old Spotted Dog. Volunteers prepared for the club's first game, a friendly against the Wanderers, and it would prepare Clapton Community for what they should expect. While there wasn't a soul in sight 15 minutes before the game, a queue formed at kick-off and stretched to the car park. Nearly 250 supporters watched that first match and now hundreds of fans attended Clapton's fixtures.

'It was Jock Stein, the celebrated Celtic manager, who coined the phrase "football is nothing without fans". For us as a club, it could not be truer. Our fans and members are the very lifeblood of the club. CCFC is owned and run by the fans. As Stuart Purcell, the assistant manager, says, "The fans are the club, we are just the add-ons",' said Price.

The committee had chosen Walthamstow as their base, joining Walthamstow FC as tenants at Wadham Lodge. Although they would have preferred to play where their roots lie in Forest Gate, with limited football facilities available and needing somewhere to start, a home across east London suited the club.

Price said, 'Clapton Community were formally formed at a members' meeting in June 2018. At the time, we did not have any management team, squad or league to play in, let alone a ground. What we did have though was passion and various talented individuals who were determined to make the idea of forming and owning a football club work. Within a few weeks we were ready. We needed to be as close as possible to our spiritual home, the Old Spotted Dog, but options were severely limited with all grounds in the east London area unavailable due to ground-sharing. Luckily, there was a pitch available adjacent to the main pitch at the Matchday Centre in Walthamstow. The main pitch at the time was shared by Essex Senior League clubs Walthamstow and Leyton Athletic. We had found a temporary home, soon to be called the Stray Dog, and made it our own by building a stand. Within a year, we were playing on the main pitch as Leyton Athletic vacated, with our newly formed women's team taking the men's place on the Stray Dog.'

Clapton didn't follow the structure of the vast majority of clubs in non-league. They weren't run by an owner and a chairman but instead followed the less common option of being a fan-run club as a committee made the decisions. This meant the committee had total control over the club and the decisions that affected every aspect of it. One of those decisions was to not have sponsorship deals.

'It's a member club. One share is one vote, with the right to vote on important issues. The decision was taken not to have outside sponsorship. It was rightly argued that a sponsor may try to exert some undue influence. It could also be argued that our 1,400 members are our sponsors,' said Price.

Sophie Axlesson was an integral part of the women's setup at Clapton, playing as a goalkeeper. She understood what the club was about and knew exactly what they wanted to achieve on and off the pitch. The women's team had come just over a year after the formation of the club, as the first team at AFC Stoke Newington had come over to play under the community banner.

'The women's team immediately and enthusiastically bought into the club's ethos and are an integral part of the club adding a further dimension to it and increasing female participation. There is an excellent relationship between the women's and men's teams, with fantastic mutual support at the respective matches,' said Axlesson.

During the 2019/20 season, the men's side found themselves fourth in the league, but with games in hand they were still in contention for the league title.

Price said, 'When the season was cancelled in March, we were ten points behind league leaders Brentham with three games in hand. We felt we had a good chance of winning the title. After a sluggish start, winning only one of our opening five games, we proceeded to go on a run of eight wins in the 12 games that followed, putting us in contention. The previous season had also seen us build momentum from a slow start. By winning eight of the final nine games during that season, we came from behind to win the title on the last day of the season. Incidentally, this was the first time we had been top all season.'

'In 2018/19, a heavy defeat to Stonewall [4-0] was the prelude to the run that saw us take the title. This season a similar defeat to Cricklewood Wanderers [5-0] preceded the run that took us to the top. The squad, the majority of which had played last season, had the know-how and experience of how to deal with the pressure and expectation of a title challenge.'

Unlike the men's side, 2019/20 had seen the newly formed women's team struggling for form and finding themselves towards the bottom of the table. Although they were off the pace compared to their male counterparts, it wasn't entirely worrying for the club.

Price continued, 'Before becoming Clapton CFC Women, the team had won promotion to Division One of the Greater London Women's Football League [in 2018/19] under the Stoke Newington name. Of course, we knew the opposition would be tougher, but we had started strongly, with a great performance in the extra preliminary round of the FA Women's Cup, as well as making a solid start in the league. Whilst the move to Clapton saw us attract a lot of new players, we also had a lot of injury issues, particular our first-choice keeper, but also the previous season's top scorer.

'We felt that the results didn't always represent the games. There is always a growing frustration when your team doesn't win. As a team, we felt that there was something not working, so we decided to part ways with our manager, and handle the last few games of the season on our own, as we had done for the past few seasons. Our team is filled with passion, skill and, above all else, grit. We knew we had a tough task ahead of us, but we won comfortably on the final day of the season. It is also worth noting that we weren't able to play a lot of our games due to the weather, and that the teams we did play were the ones in the top half of the table. Above all else though, the 2019/20 season was fantastic for us in the women's first team. We've had regular crowds at both home and away games. With Clapton CFC, women's football gets the attention, support, and encouragement it deserves. We can't wait to see what the next few seasons have in store!'

* * *

Upton Park Ladies were founded in 2020 but manager Daniel Merrix was keen to point out they had nothing to do with the historic Upton Park FC. The original men's side had first been founded over a century before Daniel had even considered the idea of forming a ladies' team and were amateurs who were considered one of the 'originals'. They were one of the 15 sides that took part in the first edition of the FA Cup in 1871/72, just five years after they were founded. Although they didn't ever win the competition, they did later win a gold medal during the 1900 Paris Olympic Games while representing Great Britain, and they were also the inaugural winners of the London Senior Cup in 1882/83. Though they were amateur, they played a huge part in football turning professional when they confronted the issue of Preston North End paying their players when the sides met in the FA Cup. At the time, Preston were disqualified from the competition, but the FA allowed clubs to start paying their players the following year in fear that they would pull away their affiliation. With such history in mind, it was important for the club to recognise the team before them as they embarked on a new chapter.

'We are in no way affiliated to the men's side so this is a completely new club,' Merrix explained. 'Although we are independent, we choose to recognise the history of the men's side that graced the football pitch before us.'

The women's game had come a long way since it was banned by the Football Association and the majority of women's sides benefited from the support of their male counterparts since its resurrection in England, but Merrix was keen to build an independent and self-reliant operation that didn't rely on the finances or resources of a men's club. In doing so, Upton Park Ladies knew they needed to provide their own kits, commercial structure and the best facilities they could. The club hadn't just been created for football either. Merrix's belief was that beyond the white lines of the football pitch, he could help build a community off it.

'Without question, we want to stand for and with the diversity of our city here in London. We want to be a leading example of what a football club for women should be like. I hope over the years to come, the success for us is a reflection of the development of myself and everyone involved as individuals. We believe and stand for the personal development and will continue to push our members to dedicate their off-field lives to develop themselves along with the help of some of our key sponsors. We feel developing people is our mission.

'The building blocks to the community feeling around the club began by aligning ourselves with charities and organisations that have been contributing to the local community for years. Once we made it clear to all we were prepared to get behind these causes, we started to attract like-minded people into key roles. This encouraged local players to get involved because we stood for something more than football, aiming to make a real difference for the people in our borough and surrounding areas.'

Merrix and other people involved in running the club knew that it would be a challenge to get more girls involved. Equality in the game was a key issue that needed to be addressed at the very top, but Merrix wanted to try and make a difference at grassroots level. In encouraging equality, he hoped he would drive more girls to get involved with the project. He and his assistant took different steps to get out into the world and encourage aspiring footballers to join them.

He said, 'It's all about positive reinforcement. There's one thing to be aware of the challenge [women's football faces] but it's another thing to be consumed by them. We, as a club, will always have our glass half full and no matter how much that affects us negatively, we will navigate through with more optimism. We try to enforce that positivity into every session with every player and give them enough room to make mistakes and learn. Often, people don't take chances as they fear failure but it's the persistence during failure that brings the wins and positive results on and off the pitch. For me, positivity always wins.

'I and my assistant coach started with the extreme lengths of old-school flyers. We went door to door to introduce ourselves and the club. From the moment the club was created, it was always our intention to build a brand that became a club, and this was part of our strategy. The next phase was social media marketing which I had some previous experience with. Running a paid advertisement was the perfect execution as it delivered over 50 per cent of our trialists. The 30 per cent that came from the flyers shouldn't be mocked either because we've had some exceptional talent come through. Most weeks we get enquiries from new players interested in joining our club and we even get parents wanting to sign their children up for future seasons.'

Merrix had the dual aim of success on the pitch and also building the community side of the club. Having a strong relationship with the local community would be important and a win-win for both parties. They both offered different expertise that would benefit their counterpart.

Upton Park Ladies had signed sponsorship deals with charities and organisations within their local community: Mind in Tower Hamlets and Newham, a charity that campaigns to help those who suffer with mental health difficulties; Food4All, which provides hot meals to those who are less fortunate; and Newham Music, an organisation that provides a musical education and hub for young people. The main focus off the pitch was to promote these organisations. Merrix had expected it to be tough to find sponsors but he felt that a lot had been achieved in such a short space of time.

'I believe we have brought an incredible amount of energy and enthusiasm to the sponsorship negotiations and have seen no difficulty in securing some great sponsors. I think it's been extremely positive not to have the backing of a men's side, but we understand the importance of some teams having the support of their men's counterparts. The more notable issue is trying to convince the in-convincible that female football has a place in the world,' he continued, with a brief pause. 'I would rather utilise my time with potential sponsors that already have a willingness and openness to the conversation of equality. I believe in life; we find what we are looking for if we search hard enough.

'The lockdowns [at the end of the 2019/20 and 2020/21 seasons] gave us an opportunity to focus on supporting Mind. They were massive contributors to getting us off the ground and the fantastic work around mental health was something our community needed at such a difficult time during the pandemic. Our next mission is to help Food4All in replacing their delivery vans that supply warm foods to the homeless, but we'd also like to launch our own personal charity to distribute funds to a variety of causes throughout the year.'

Ahead of their inaugural season in the Greater London Women's Football League, Upton Park Ladies needed a home. They managed to secure a place at the West Ham United Foundation, a ground that suited their community needs. The foundation does a huge amount for the local community and Merrix was well aware of this factor when he organised a lease of the 3G pitch.

'The foundation do some unbelievable work for the local community as part of their partnership with West Ham United Football Club. The ground is home to their academies for both the boys' and girls' teams so it's a catalyst to the development of local people within the game.

Upton Park Ladies looked for inspirations across all levels of women's football in England. Clubs like Millwall Lionesses, Bowers & Pitsea Ladies, Tottenham Hotspur Women and West Ham Women gave them the inspiration they sought on and off the pitch.

Merrix said, 'I've enjoyed looking into the likes of Millwall [Lionesses] and the way they are building on and off the pitch. Our friends Bowers & Pitsea are doing a fantastic job that is worth recognition and none of this comes with the riches of the Women's Super League level so it's truly inspiring to me. We are connected with such great clubs as friends that we can learn from, on how we develop people and players whilst being competitive on a low budget and even self-sustaining. You can often find inspiration from grassroots level right to the very top. I think we all put pressure on people to turn us into a West Ham or Spurs and there is not enough recognition for the smaller clubs doing it right.'

There is no doubt that one day, Merrix has ambitions to manage at the very top or even take Upton Park Ladies as high as he can, but it's also important to him for people to appreciate the grassroots and smaller clubs. Upton Park were put in Division Two North of the Greater London Women's Football League ahead of the 2020/21 season. As their inaugural season, it was only right to focus on structure and stability before they could dream of moving up the pyramid. For Merrix, that meant working with the sponsors to overcome any changes they might have faced while going into the season with a squad that could build up throughout the year.

'We are positive, but we also remain realistic. Our first season will be for us to get our house in order, so to speak, meaning we are looking at going into the season with a full-strength squad and good numbers, so we are not left short on a matchday. The hardest year for the club is always the first year with the financial outlay being higher, but we have some incredible sponsors to make it [playing the first season] a reality. The club has the ability to go big, but we must walk before we can run. We are just a grassroots club, and a lot of sides think too big, too early. Our ambition at this point is to see through the season whilst challenging and we would like to become a feeder club for those bigger sides, developing players to have careers in the beautiful game.'

Upton Park Ladies made a dream start to their first campaign with a big win but soon found it tough, with several defeats on the bounce. The opening-day victory had come at home to Alexandra Park Women, 8-1, before defeats to New London Lionesses Development Women, Brentford Women Development, Hackney Women Reserves and Hackney Lionesses, sending the club on an unwanted four-game losing streak. Although they had been in a bad run of form, a goalless draw against Regents Park Women and a 1-1 draw with Forest Crusaders Ladies put them five points clear of the bottom of the table when the season was halted.

The inconsistency wasn't unexpected, but Merrix knew there was plenty of room for improvement.

'As expected, it was a season of development, growth and adaptation. On the field, I believe when you build slowly and in a calculated manner, you can keep a healthy and positive culture,' he explained. 'We started off with an 8-1 victory in our opening game which seemed like a perfect start for a new club but, on reflection, it was a false perception of the way the first half of the season would go. We've had some hard moments since our inception, but I like to constantly remind the squad that it's through losses and struggles that we grow together. The last couple of games had seen us really tighten up the defence after some key signings mid-season, and I think we could have kicked on going into the second half of the campaign.'

11

Playing the Field

BECKY SHEPHARD made the switch ahead of the 2020/21 season from Harlow Town Ladies to Stevenage Women, going up a level to the FA Women's National League in the process. Although she had enjoyed her short time with the Hawks, she felt it was the right time to seek a new challenge and fulfil her ambitions.

'It's never an easy decision to leave the club that you enjoy and have made friendships at, but for me, I knew I wasn't getting any younger,' she explained. 'I wanted to keep challenging myself in what I felt I had left of my career. Everyone knows the National League is a very good standard, so to be offered the opportunity to be able to play in the league was not only an honour but a decision I couldn't take lightly. We [Harlow] were on the verge of joining the same league, but that didn't happen, so I had to make the decision that was right for me.'

Shephard had only been at Harlow for a season after joining in the summer of 2019. She hadn't planned to move on so quickly but made the decision during the following summer. As a forward, she had great fortune in Essex as she netted 26 goals in 19 appearances with seven games of the season still to play. It was no easy feat but what she achieved certainly got Stevenage's attention.

Boro needed to strengthen their squad. Since their promotion from the Eastern Region Women's Football League Premier Division in 2015/16 they had struggled in the FA Women's National League (the then Women's Premier League). In their four seasons in the fourth tier of women's football, the highest they had finished was a respectable sixth, but even then they had found themselves 26 points off the title-winning MK Dons Women. They were never close to going back down, despite finishing 11th out of 12 sides in their first season, when they were still nine points above Lowestoft Town Ladies; while they finished ninth in 2018/19, 11 points from safety but a massive 32 points off the title; and found themselves tenth during 2019/20 after 15 games but already 24 points off the title challenge before the season was ended early. Stevenage were hoping that the addition of Shephard would boost their chances of competing higher up the league.

Shephard said, 'I joined Harlow for the 2019/20 season after having a season at a club where I completely fell out of love with the sport. I knew myself that I wasn't ready to give up football, so it was important that I picked the right team in order to regain the love I had for the game and to remember why I started playing. I couldn't thank Harlow enough for giving me the platform to do that.'

The impressive season with the Hawks had been a bonus as the team were close to promotion to the National League, but as a forward Shephard was pleased with her ability to find the back of the net regularly. It was what she looked to do before the season had kicked off, but to score over 20 goals was great on a personal level for her.

'As a striker, you're always judged on your goalscoring tally so to have a good season goal-wise was definitely a great feeling. It was a season of wanting to be able to enjoy my football again and scoring the goals definitely helped towards that.'

Shephard's time at Harlow had been great for her confidence. Manager Dean Perrett had given her the freedom to express herself on the pitch and play her game. For any player, that was all they could ask for and it contributed to her scoring tally.

'At Harlow, it was a mixture of the style of play and the players I was around. We played some good football throughout the season and that reflected in the fact we were sat top of the table, but there were also many talented players in the team too. I was given the freedom I desired and was allowed to play my game which gives any player a confidence boost, especially when the manager believes in them enough to play that role, and again, I think that reflects in why I had a successful season.'

Shephard's career had taken in a broad spectrum of sides as she had been at Bedwell Rangers, Tottenham Hotspur, Cisco College, Hertford, Royston Town and Cambridge United before her move to Harlow in 2019. This meant she fulfilled her childhood dream of playing football, something she had decided from a very early age, as she looked to pursue the sport as much as time would allow.

'I've always wanted to play,' Shephard said. 'When I was five or six years old, I used to always pester my dad to take me to football with him and the same with my brother's football. I took up playing myself when I was seven or eight and never looked back. Football's always been a big part of my life. It's literally all I know!

'From a young age, I've taken my football seriously because, as I said, it's all I knew and what I wanted to pursue further. When I signed for Spurs at 11 years of age, that's when I truly started to look at football differently. It was an unreal platform for any player wanting to progress and improve.'

Out of all the clubs Shephard has played for, each has influenced her game in a unique way. As a Spurs fan all her life, it was a privilege to have worn the same white shirt as her heroes.

'From my own personal career, I think every team I've played for has had a positive impact and influence on me in some shape or form. That's the best thing about football, you never stop learning and you can never learn too much. Every team had their own philosophies and ambitions as a club, so that had helped with my learning as a player to adapt and contribute to their individual successes.

'Being a Tottenham fan, it was an absolute honour to pull on the shirt. Every kid dreams of representing the club they support, and I was lucky enough to be able to do that for seven seasons. I was also fortunate to have a stint with the first team, and some of the lessons I learnt from being around such highly talented players will stick with me for the rest of my career.'

After making her way through several youth sides at Tottenham, playing for the thirds and first team, Shephard played the majority of her football in the Eastern Region Women's Football League, tier five of the pyramid. She featured for Hertford in 2016/17, scoring six goals in the 18 games she played as the Blues finished eighth, before she found her way to the Premier Division the following season as she signed for Royston. Her spell with the Crows had been far better despite the club finishing mid-table as she netted 24 goals in 23 games.

Shephard's reward for impressive form saw her rise up the pyramid to the FA Women's National League Division One South East, the league she had returned to with Stevenage, as she signed for Cambridge United Women ahead of the 2018/19 season. With the U's, she scored just nine times in 31 appearances as they finished eighth before she felt the move to Harlow would benefit her career. The switch to the Hawks had seen her drop down a tier back to the Premier Division of the Eastern Region League. Although she flourished, it was more of a coincidence that she kept finding herself in that particular league rather than her choosing it to suit her level.

'I think it's more of a coincidence, to be honest. I've played for teams that have been relegated into the Eastern Region and, likewise, I've played for sides that have worked their way up to it through promotion. The standard is of a very high level and some of the players could easily go and play higher, so it never fazed me that I played in that league for a fair bit as it still challenges you to improve.'

Shephard had spent her whole career as a striker, but she could have just as easily found a love for a different role at a young age. With the influences of her dad and brother she could have been shaped into a defender or even a goalkeeper, but she opted to be a forward instead.

'It's funny because, as I said, I grew up loving the game because of my family. My dad was a goalkeeper, and my brother a defender, so you would've thought I'd follow in their footsteps, but instead, I naturally drifted towards being a striker. It worked a treat when we used to go over the field for a kickabout as youngsters. I'd always go up against them. I remember the feeling of either beating them and scoring or, if I didn't, the feeling of learning what I could've done better. It sounds silly, but I owe a lot to them little sessions we had as a family.'

Women's football has certainly progressed since it was unbanned in 1971, but opportunities for Shephard and her peers remained sparse until more recent times. But still to this day, rarely are players in the Women's Super League and Championship signed to clubs on a professional basis. Shephard found herself wondering where she could have been had women's football developed in a different way prior to her involvement, but she was grateful she still had the opportunity to play the game.

'Women's football has come a long way since I started playing. Back when I first started out, it was mainly all boys that played so it was hard to find a decent level of women's football of fully committed players. Opportunities were few and far between back in the day, but every season that passes, you can see the foundations of how big women's football is becoming and will continue to become. The future for the sport is very exciting but there is still a long way to go.

'Growing up, I knew it would be nothing but hard work to open the opportunities I gained. I'm thankful I still live by that ethos today, but it's really up to the players individually and how badly they want to succeed. I was quite fortunate at school that I naturally got on with the boys because of football, so I was always spending every lunch break and after school playing a game amongst them. Some of them to this day are very supportive of my football career and always take an interest in what I'm doing and who I'm playing for.'

Shephard's focus had become firmly on her new club, Stevenage. Going up to the National League from the Eastern Region Women's Football League for her was a great opportunity to develop with a top club. She had been welcomed with open arms, which was all she could ask for, but she knew she still had to work hard to achieve what she wanted. If Stevenage could gain promotion, she knew she would be one division off the FA Women's Championship, but it wouldn't be that easy. If she focused on her game, who knew where her playing career would take her.

'I've really enjoyed my time at Stevenage so far. The management, coaching staff and all the girls have been unreal. It has been a welcoming environment from the offset. There is a real good family vibe within the squad and when I joined, the foundations of the club and the philosophy is something that I brought into which is important as part of a player's progression. I feel like my game will be taken to the next level and there's some really good things to come from this club, which I'm excited about.

'The standard of the National League is exceptional. Any player, manager or coach in that league will tell you the same. As much as I fell out of love with the game and it didn't go as I had hoped, I learnt some valuable lessons that will stay with me forever. This time around playing for Stevenage, I'm absolutely loving football, and it's great to be able to really test myself in a good league against some talented players.'

With a second chance to do well in the National League after her spell with Cambridge hadn't gone as well as she wished, Shephard knew exactly how she would have to apply herself to her football if she was going to make the most of the opportunity.

'As a player, my focus is to always just push myself to be the best version of the player that I know I can be. I always try to make my next training session or my next match the best one because football careers only last so long. It's important to make the most of every moment. On a personal level, my family play a huge part. They've put in hours, money, support, and love into my career from the start, so it has been unconditional. I want to give back to them by ensuring I perform to my best standards every time I play. That is very important to me.'

* * *

At the age of 27, Charlie Mann found himself signing for Essex Senior League side Walthamstow. The appointment of Max Mitchell by the east London club had convinced him that Stow was his next destination, joining over halfway through the 2019/20 season. With the departure of the previous manager, the squad was depleted and needed an injection of new talent. Mann wasn't the only one to sign but he knew he would be the first-choice goalkeeper upon his arrival.

'He [Mitchell] was a key factor for me joining Walthamstow. He is a good friend of mine and had got the job at Walthamstow. I played with and for him, and I knew he was joining a big club that were looking to be successful. It was exciting to be part of what they wanted to achieve. I also knew a few players also signing for the club,' Mann said. 'Jason Beck, Frazer John, Dan Ferrigno and Tommy Fletcher, who I'm good friends with, were in the same position. Max wanted me there so the transition was smooth.'

Mann's footballing career hadn't been smooth, nor had it seen him spend too long at each club he represented. He had been a goalkeeper since the age of eight and started his career in the Arsenal academy.

'Everyone had their own story [of how they joined an academy], but I feel mine was quite unique. I was playing for a Sunday side in Harlow, and one of the coaches, Rodney Clements, asked me which side I supported. I had told him it was Arsenal and he pulled out this card. It was an official Arsenal scout's card and he told me that he had just been taken on as an official scout. He wanted to take me on a trial, but it was a case of seeing how things would go. I wasn't expecting much. Rodney managed to get me a trial. I trained, played and got to know the squad before, at the end of the 2002/03 season, they signed me on a one-year deal which, as a nine- or ten-year-old, was pretty special.

'When I was younger, I played outfield, but I wouldn't say I was very good. I have played in goal since I was eight, so you could say I have been playing in goal all my life.'

During his time with Arsenal, Mann was a part of their 2008/09 FA Youth Cup-winning side. Their run had seen them beat top teams on their way to winning the competition. Arsenal had begun away to Aston Villa in the third round as clubs from the Premier League and Championship entered. They were 3-2 victors before hosting Wolverhampton Wanderers in the fourth round, picking up a 3-1 win. The fifth round was another away trip, this time to the north-east to face Sunderland. The young Gunners eased past them with a 4-0 win before they faced a game closer to home against Tottenham Hotspur in the quarter-finals. After a 3-1 victory over their north London rivals on the road, Arsenal faced holders Manchester City.

As the competition got to the semi-finals, the format changed and the sides would play each other over two legs. The first was played at the City of Manchester Stadium, with Arsenal winning 2-1. They had found themselves 1-0 down as Alex Nimely scored for the hosts, but goals from Jay Emmanuel-Thomas and Gilles Sunu gave them the advantage when they welcomed City back to the Emirates for the second leg. In front of a crowd of just over 9,000 supporters, Arsenal eased past the Citizens with a 4-1 scoreline (6-2 on aggregate) as a Sanchez Watt double and goals from Jack Wilshere and Kyle Bartley were enough. In the other semi-final, Liverpool had beaten Birmingham City, winning 6-1 on aggregate to set up a huge final.

The final was also a two-legged affair as Arsenal stepped out against Liverpool at the Emirates in the first leg in front of over 33,000 supporters. They lined up with players who had made it to the first team – Emmanuel Frimpong, Francis Coquelin and Jack Wilshere – and the quality was enough as they took a 4-1 win over the Reds into the second leg. That game was played at Anfield, but in front of a lower crowd of 7,792. The Gunners were in control, although they didn't need to fear Liverpool as they picked up a 2-1 win to beat their opponents 6-2 on aggregate. It was Arsenal's seventh FA Youth Cup, and for any young player to be involved, it was a great experience.

Mann said, 'It was brilliant. I was only 16 at the time so it was a great experience. I played at a few professional grounds, so for a young player, that was huge.'

Mann hadn't made it on to the pitch during the FA Youth Cup run, although he found himself in the squad for the majority of the matches. It was disappointing for him, as any player would have loved to have contributed on the pitch, but instead he featured in a few games in the Premier Academy League. Arsenal won the double in 2008/09 as they lifted the FAPL championship. They had comfortably won Group A, finishing 25 points ahead of second-placed Norwich City, to make it through to the play-off semi-finals. Tottenham Hotspur, Manchester City and Sunderland had finished top of the other three groups as they also reached the play-offs.

The structure of the competition meant clubs in the ten-team group played each other twice before also playing ten inter-group fixtures, meaning the final group tables were decided after each team had played 28 games. The winners of the groups progressed to the semi-finals before the winners contested a national final for the title. Arsenal faced another trip to Manchester and again played at the City of Manchester Stadium as they beat their hosts 2-1. Rhys Murphy and Cedric Evina scored for the Gunners while Spurs were victorious against Sunderland as Ryan Mason and Andros Townsend were on target for the other north London side. Just over 5,000 spectators travelled to Tottenham for the final, witnessing Arsenal's Murphy score the only goal of the game as they lifted the title at White Hart Lane.

Mann said, 'I didn't make an appearance [in the cup], unfortunately. I was only a sub but didn't get the chance to play on the pitch, but I witnessed some fantastic games. I was in the squad that went to Villa Park in the third round before we played Wolves at the Underhill Stadium. I was left out of the squad against Sunderland, so didn't travel up north, but I was back when we faced Tottenham at White Hart Lane. They had a really strong squad with the likes of John Bostock and Andros Townsend. I also found myself on the bench for both the semi-final and final, and although I didn't get on the pitch, it brought some special memories and memories I will treasure forever.

'I played four games that year for the under-18s, featuring against Norwich, Ipswich and Portsmouth. I was only 16 at the time but playing in a really strong team.'

Mann didn't get the chance to join the Gunners' professional ranks, but he played alongside players who did achieve the childhood dream. Jack Wilshere went on to play for both Arsenal and England at senior level while also playing for Bolton Wanderers, Bournemouth and West Ham United. He has made over 300 appearances for club and country, an incredible achievement for anyone.

'Wilshere was probably one of the best players that I played with. Jack was a year older but was born in the same year, so he used to come down and play with us. He was a standout player from a young age, and we used to get on really well. You always knew he was going to go on and make the most of his career. Injuries blighted him, but he had the ability to be one of the best players the country has ever produced.'

Despite being offered a contract extension at Arsenal, Mann opted to leave north London and head south to Crystal Palace as an apprentice. It was a decision he felt he needed to make as he dropped down the pecking order within the Gunners' youth setup.

'I wasn't given much of a choice,' he explained. 'I was offered a two-year scholarship, but I was given the understanding that they'd be bringing in another goalkeeper and I wouldn't play as many games. After a meeting with Liam Brady, I had a chat with my parents and made the decision to leave. The phone was ringing quite a bit, but I chose Palace as my best fit.'

Mann spent a couple of years at Palace and made the first-team squad a few times, finding himself on the bench in both the FA Cup and Championship. Mann was a substitute against the likes of Watford, Sheffield United and Middlesbrough during the 2009/10 season as well as the FA Cup ties against Wolves and Aston Villa, before making the squad against Watford and Middlesbrough the following season. He didn't make an appearance, however, and soon found his time at Palace coming to an end as he was released.

'It's not a nice experience for anyone [being released],' Mann said. 'Football can change very quickly when new managers or owners come in. I played a couple of reserve games at Brentford and some games for Stevenage, but I had to think what was next for me.'

As he struggled to find a professional club to sign for, Mann dropped down the pyramid and into non-league. He had been asked to come in at Croydon Athletic and decided to give it a go as he just wanted to play football.

'I didn't have many options, but I still had aspirations of playing league football. I had contact with someone at non-league level who put me in touch with Croydon. I played ten to 12 games for them, which was good experience of first-team football.'

While it was his first real experience of non-league and senior football, Mann's time at Croydon was overshadowed by the financial situation at the club. Croydon played in the Isthmian League Division One South, with the players battling more than three points on the pitch. A property developer who had taken over in 2008 had been investigated by HM Revenue and Customs due to allegations that he had bought the club for money-laundering. The manager and assistant manager left due to the investigations and fixtures weren't able to be fulfilled. During this period, many players began to transfer to other teams.

Mann said, 'I received a call one Friday to say their [Croydon's] keeper had let them down, so I started at the club by filling in. I was only 18 at the time, but my first game ended 0-0 against Burgess Hill. When their keeper returned, they didn't get back in touch, but when he wasn't available again, they called me back. I didn't mind going back because all I wanted to do was play football. It was a young side, so it was great to be involved, and when I look back at my time, it was a great experience.

'They didn't have a lot of money and there were a few players that were owed money. We were told that if we couldn't fulfil our fixtures, the club would face severe penalties. Many of the players didn't want to put in the miles on travel because the [Isthmian] league at the time meant there were a lot of long journeys. When players left, it became an apparent everyone would leave at some point.'

Croydon received a hefty fine and a ten-point deduction after they were found to have breached FA rules. As the year came closer to its end, they were unable to fulfil a fixture against Ramsgate and stated they wouldn't be able to go ahead with the following weekend's game either. With financial troubles and players having opted to leave, the club eventually folded during the 2011/12 season. Those who hadn't left had to find a new home and Charlie opted to join his hometown club, Harlow Town.

Mann's time at Harlow didn't see him feature on the pitch. He had been signed as a back-up keeper and wasn't needed, and he didn't feel his time at Harlow was anything special.

'I played for Harlow because they were local to me at the time. It was a club I knew about and they offered me the opportunity. Having the number-one spot in non-league is difficult and every team was reluctant to put a young keeper between the sticks. I wasn't known in non-league as I hadn't had a full season under my belt. I don't think I made an appearance. The club were doing well but they weren't really delivering on a top-level stage, and that season, we missed out on the play-offs. It was nice to join the club as it was in my hometown, but it was nothing beyond that. I didn't feel a sense of nostalgia.'

After his time at Harlow had come to an end, Mann headed to Sweden to continue his career. As an apprentice at Crystal Palace he was also involved in a league education programme where he was looked after, and one way they supported young footballers was by helping them find opportunities abroad. Mann had a spell in Sweden at a fourth-tier club.

'I spent three months in Sweden playing for Anundsjö IF and enjoyed my time there, but it was in the northern part of Sweden, so it was a bit desolate. I didn't find it particularly tough as I felt I was mature for my age. I wasn't fazed about being out of my comfort zone and the biggest issue was that it was in a rural part of Sweden so that was different, and I didn't see as much as game time as I had hoped. The language barrier was a bit of an issue, but the majority of players and staff spoke decent English, so it wasn't the biggest issue. When my contract ended, my flights were already booked, so it made sense to head back [to England]. Although I enjoyed my time, I wouldn't have stayed longer or rushed back.'

When Mann returned to England, he had spells at Waltham Abbey, Sevenoaks Town and Hadley. The opportunity at Abbey really presented itself for Mann before he had moved on to Sevenoaks.

'I caught wind that Abbey were looking for a number-two goalkeeper, so I went down for pre-season. In the first game of pre-season, the first-choice keeper was injured. When the keeper called it a day [due to the injury], they took me on as the number one but it wasn't my best football. The manager agreed it wasn't my best spell and it wasn't working out, so I didn't play for the rest of the season.

'I got a phone call from Micky Hazard who was at Sevenoaks Town. I was a student at the time so didn't have much going on. I felt I had matured from Abbey and I really enjoyed my time at the club. It had given me a route into non-league football, and it was a really nice community club.'

Once Mann's time at Sevenoaks came to a conclusion at the end of the 2013/14 season, he signed for Hadley and spent three seasons with the Bricks.

'I owe a lot to Hadley,' he said. 'I hold them very close to my heart. I had a fantastic experience there over three years and the people at the club are fantastic. We had a good side and had a great FA Cup run during one of the seasons [2016/17]. I think that is where I would like to finish my playing career if things work out.'

Mann made just under 100 appearances over the three seasons, including reaching the FA Cup third qualifying round. They squeezed through the first three rounds, beating Brantham Athletic in the extra preliminary round, Hertford Town in the preliminary round, and London Colney in the first qualifying round, all by 1-0 scorelines, before they beat Kings Langley 2-1 in the second qualifying round. They travelled to Eastbourne Borough in the third qualifying round but the game ended goalless, so the teams met at Hadley's Brickfield Lane for a replay which the visitors won 4-1.

Mann really enjoyed his time at the Bricks but for the 2017/18 season, he made the switch to Hertford, where in his first season they finished 15th in the Isthmian League North Division, before they were transferred to the South Central Division. They struggled in 2018/19 as they finished 18th and avoided relegation by three points. He briefly returned to Hadley, who were playing in the Spartan South Midlands League during that season, after he found himself out of favour at Hertford, before moving to Tring Athletic in 2019/20.

'I left Hertford after a new manager came in and didn't want anyone from the old regime. Max [Mitchell] had found his way in at Tring [as a player] and there, the manager was asking about me. They were putting together a decent squad and I knew a few of the lads already at the club. We thought it would go quite well should it have continued as we were top of the league in October 2019.'

Tring had been fighting with Colney Heath for the Spartan South Midlands League Premier Division title while they tried to keep Biggleswade Town at bay. Colney Heath had sat top for much of the season, but Tring were clinging on to them while Biggleswade were still in contention. Although they were fighting for promotion, feelings turned sour behind the scenes, with many players unhappy at what was happening.

Mann said, 'Behind the scenes, players were not overly happy. I went to work one Wednesday as normal and found out the manager had been sacked. Many players followed suit and I was left out of the squad for the next game. In my search for a new club, Max had become the manager at Walthamstow [midway through the 2019/20 season] and after a conversation, it was a simple case of me wanting to be there.'

Mann signed for Stow as first-choice keeper during their battle for the championship. The Essex Senior League title race was between three teams as Saffron Walden, who sat top after playing an additional three games, were being chased down by Hashtag United and Walthamstow. Mann made a great impact when he first signed, helping the club to important wins against Takeley and Saffron Walden, while almost helping Stow on to wins against Hashtag. He was not fazed at coming in during such a crucial stage of the season.

'I knew Max was at a big club and a club that were looking to be successful, and I was very excited to play a part in what they wanted to achieve. I didn't feel any pressure coming in during the season.'

Although Mann had made a great start to life in a Stow shirt, once he returned for the 2020/21 season he struggled for form. Pre-season had seen Walthamstow lose four of their six fixtures, while they had dropped points against Stansted and Southend Manor at home due to goalkeeping errors. By October, Mann had found himself out of the squad and struggled to get minutes on the pitch before he was moved on.

'When I joined towards the end of last season [2019/20], I felt I was playing well and there was loads of confidence within. I felt on top of my game. My performance at Saffron Walden was very good but I don't think the lockdown helped me and it knocked me off my stride. I felt a little disjointed through pre-season and I couldn't pinpoint what the problem was, but I didn't feel the same as I had done previously. You are always going to go through bad spells and, for me, that happened to have come at Walthamstow.'

The club moved Mann on rather than keeping him on the bench and Mitchell said in the next matchday programme that a player of his quality needed to be playing. In search of a new club, Mann found himself back at Hadley sooner than he had expected, but it was a no-brainer to rejoin the Bricks.

'I had significant interest from other clubs within the ESL [Essex Senior League] as well as the Spartan South [Midlands] League, but I had always had close links to Hadley. I've held them very close to my heart and they were really good to me during my time. After speaking to the club, it was a fairly easy decision to go back as I'm well known, and they have a brilliant manager at the club. It was where I wanted to be.'

12

The Rise of the Wanderers

IN SEPTEMBER 1999, Dorking Wanderers were founded by Marc White. His beloved Wimbledon were free-falling towards Premier League relegation, so the wearied supporter decided to do something with his Saturdays. With thoughts running through his mind, his solution was to build a team of his own with a few mates, making the most of his weekends in the process.

'I was bored of watching Premier League football,' he said. 'I thought it would be more socially fun to create a football team myself. It was just a few mates getting together and having a laugh.'

They began in the now-extinct Crawley and District Football League for their first season before making the sideways movement to Division Four of the West Sussex League. They won Division Four on their first attempt before being promoted to Division Three, finishing as runners-up in 2001/02, which was enough to earn promotion to Division Two, where they spent two seasons before eventually going up again.

Having won Division Two of the West Sussex Football League in 2003/04, White led his side into Division One. They spent two seasons there before winning promotion to the Premier Division after finishing third in 2005/06. The following season, they won yet another title and earned another promotion as they won the Premier Division at their first attempt, becoming champions on the final day. Dorking were then promoted to the Southern Combination, starting in Division Three.

The Southern Combination was a tough one to begin with and Dorking spent four seasons in the Third Division before they reached the Second Division. In 2010/11 Dorking were Division Three champions, having begun their journey, and they continued their hot streak of promotions. It had been an incredible run but White certainly didn't expect to be so successful in such a short space of time.

'No, not really,' he said when asked if they had expected their rapid rise. 'We seemed to have got a bit of an appetite for it [promotion], which still burns within the squad today. That's why I feel the club have done so well in such a short space of time. We were just a bunch of mates at the very start but as we have progressed through the leagues, we have just added better players from better leagues.'

The promotion in 2010/11 had seen them rise to Step 7 of the National League System, level 11 of the pyramid, ahead of the 2011/12 season. Dorking had officially become a senior non-league club, reaching the recognised level of the lowest-ranked outfits. After a loss on the opening day of the season against East Preston, Wanderers recorded their first win against Storrington before facing defeat soon after against Rustington. As August came to an end and September began, the club went on a seven-game winning run before they were beaten by Eastbourne United Association. That was quickly put out of their mind as November began with a 1-0 victory over Little Common before White led his players on to another decent run of form, remaining unbeaten for another seven games. That run took them into the new year before Steyning Town got the better of Wanderers. As the season went on, they recorded just two losses in 14 games and, although they tasted defeat for the seventh time against second-placed Hailsham Town, the 21 wins they racked up throughout the season were enough to finish third. That in turn meant they were promoted to Division One of the Southern Combination.

Before Dorking could play in Division One, they were denied their promotion on ground-grading rules. The criteria covered a range of items a club needed to ensure were up to standard and correct, from the boundary of the ground and capacity to floodlighting and toilets. Any clubs not meeting the correct criteria are denied promotion and teams set to be relegated can get a reprieve.

There had been an enormous amount of work by the staff at Dorking to get the ground approved. They weren't the biggest club and certainly didn't have a lot of money behind them as they sought to get the promotion they had worked hard for on the pitch. The fact they were still a very closed club made it special when they won an appeal to make the move to the Southern Combination Football League Division One (Step 5).

White said, 'At the time, we were the first club to ever successfully appeal a ground-grading decision, so we were delighted about that. It took an awful lot of work because we were essentially still a bunch of friends and funded entirely by our own pockets. We didn't have any benefactors, so everything we had done was done organically and done between people involved and local businesses. It was an enormous amount of work to get the ground up to standard.'

They initially struggled in Division One as it was a jump up from the standard they had played before. It was tough from the off as it offered promotion to the Southern and Isthmian Leagues, which was a level many clubs wanted to reach. White was no different, but Dorking had to battle through Division One if they were going to achieve that.

The first season in the division, 2012/13, had seen Dorking finish 20th, two places from the foot of the table. Worthing United had been relegated with 16 points while second-bottom AFC Uckfield Town had saved themselves from the drop by three points. Dorking were as close to relegation as their league position suggested as they won 41 points but were still 53 points off the champions, Peacehaven & Telscombe.

Ahead of the 2013/14 season, the division was reduced as 22 teams became 20. If Wanderers had not improved quickly enough then they could have found themselves closer to the bottom, but instead, they had picked up drastically and, after 38 games, they finished eighth, totalling a stronger points tally and closing the gap on the leaders to 41. Although it was still a hefty gap to overcome, there were signs of improvement and that was exactly what they needed. East Preston had won the title this time around, but Dorking were looking to achieve that the following season.

White said, 'With the standard of the league, it was a huge jump up. Probably one of the biggest jumps we had made and one of the most significant in terms of things being done more professionally. It was little things like we had to have a matchday programme.

'I think we had to just acclimatise to that Division One. The management team, at the time, needed to adjust but I needed more support. It was a case of having to scout the opposition more, scouting new players more and simply demanding more [from everyone]. I had to surround myself more with the management team and I think that was enough to see us promoted.'

The adjustment period got off to an almost perfect start as Dorking picked up ten points from their first four games before being beaten by Littlehampton Town at the start of September. A loss to Pagham was sandwiched between two wins against Loxwood and Lancing before White inspired his players on to an eight-game unbeaten run. A defeat to Newhaven was put out of their mind quickly as they remained unbeaten for 13 games, until losing to Shoreham in March. In the final month of the season, Dorking were beaten three times in ten games as they finished as runners-up. Although they had got the promotion they sought, being one of the best runners-up at Step 5, they missed out on the title by two points as Littlehampton Town reached 84 points to their 83.

Ahead of 2015/16, their first season in the Isthmian League Division One South, White hadn't expected much but after 46 games Dorking had accumulated a staggering 90 points. Although it was an incredible total, it wasn't enough for the title as Folkestone Invicta had picked up an even more impressive 114 points. With automatic promotion out of reach, Wanderers had a second chance at promotion to the Premier Division through the play-offs but faced a tough test against Faversham Town in the semi-finals. In the biggest game of their history to date, Wanderers took the lead ten minutes in as Luke Hackett finished well. The lead lasted until after the half-time break when John Scarborough levelled the game. With both sets of fans urging their team to score the winner, the Faversham faithful were delighted as Charley Robertson popped up to score in the 90th minute. The feeling of heartbreak swept around everyone at Dorking, but for White, the season had seen them do better than they had expected, and they would have another chance the following year.

The 2016/17 campaign saw Dorking finish second again, but even with 105 points they didn't get promoted automatically. Tooting & Mitcham United had also finished with 105 points but had a better goal difference by seven. For White, it had brought an astonishing feeling with what they had achieved during the season, but they still had to settle for the play-offs once more.

He said, 'I think we learnt a lot from the first season going into the second. We finished joint top with 105 points, so it was a phenomenal points tally to not get promoted. We had to go through the play-offs and the only times we've played in the Isthmian League South, we had finished second in both seasons. That was a really big accolade because the jump from the county football to the Isthmian League is a big one, but this time, we had a good structure to the club, and we were ready for the move up.'

The play-offs were to also be contested by third-placed Greenwich Borough, fourth-placed Corinthian-Casuals and fifth-placed Hastings United. Finishing as runners-up saw Wanderers face Hastings in the semi-final as they welcomed the Arrows to Westhumble Playing Fields. The tie was level after 90 minutes and extra time so went to penalties to decide who would go to the final against Corinthian-Casuals, who had won 4-3 in the other tie. Dorking won the shoot-out 4-3 to earn a place in the final, which had become the biggest game for both White and the club, but they needed to stay focused if they were to gain promotion to the Isthmian League Premier Division (Step 3).

Again they were on home turf and again a penalty shoot-out was required. Once more, Dorking were victorious and it was delight for White as he led his players into the Premier Division.

Dorking knew it would be tough at Step 3, so things needed to change as they prepared for a historical season. Ahead of 2017/18 they spent money on a player for the first time. White had already understood what was at stake and knew investment could take the club to new heights when they began life in Step 4. They also brought in another four or five players ahead of their inaugural game at Step 3.

White said, 'The first season we found that it was another huge jump and we finished lower than our usual mid-table. We decided to buy our first ever player, Jason Prior, who is still with us today, so the second season, we had brought in four or five players, and it turned out to be the best thing we had done [bringing in Prior]. We won the Premier Division, had a ground move and started to average the best part of 800 on a matchday. It was a big thing around Dorking so that's when it took off.'

The 2017/18 season saw Dorking finish 14th. They had a slow start and picked up a single win in their opening six games, while they struggled to go on a really good run of form throughout the season. Their best unbeaten run was eight games, but it didn't last for long enough to build any real traction.

In 2018/19 eyes began to gaze over in Dorking's direction. In only their second season in the Premier Division, they lifted the title after opening up a 22-point gap over Carshalton Athletic. They suffered one loss in August as they collected eight points out of a possible 15 before they began to gather momentum. As they went into September, they began a ten-game unbeaten run before suffering defeat to Haringey Borough. The loss had knocked them off balance at the end of November as they were defeated a further two times, but January marked a new spark of form as Dorking became almost unstoppable in the new year. They went 13 games unbeaten while scoring 39 goals in the process before second-placed Carshalton Athletic narrowly beat them 3-2. Despite suffering their fifth loss of the season, Dorking remained unbeaten in their final seven games as they marched towards the title with a huge margin of points to those in the play-off positions below.

The gap at the end of the season was one that was a rarity, and no one had expected it, especially White.

'We didn't expect it to go that way,' he explained, talking about the 22-point gap. 'The first season had been tough, there was no doubt, but the second season was a series of phenomenal performances and I think we had 26 clean sheets that season. The new signings had really done the job, but looking back, I can't see us having a season like that again or even topping it. The dominance was just incredible.'

The incredible rise of Wanderers had continued as they made it to National League South. Their league position had put them two promotions away from the Football League but that was not going to cross the mind of White, who understood how hard they worked just to get to Step 2. It was only going to get tougher, but they still believed they belonged at the level they had reached.

White said, 'We are really proud of the achievement. I've been here from day one but it's a massive setup off the field now and we have a good number of people who are part of the Wanderers project. You have to pinch yourself sometimes as it's been a phenomenal rise. The hard work within the club has never stopped, and I don't think we've sat down for long enough to appreciate how far we have come.

'Occasionally, we have little reminders like when we played Stockport County in the FA Trophy last season [2019/20] in the second round proper. We beat them 4-0 at their ground. You still look back and remember us playing in the Fourth Division of the Sussex League and now you are playing Stockport County who were playing Manchester City in the First Division [21 years prior]. That just shows the contrast in direction between the two sides.'

While the rise was remarkable, White had little time to sit down and admire what everyone had achieved at the club as they had a National League season to compete in. The 2019/20 campaign got off to a mixed start. Although they had won their first three games – beating Slough Town, Hemel Hempstead Town and Tonbridge Angels – they followed that with two points in five matches. It was a stark reminder of how tough the division was, but they returned to winning ways in September. With a further two defeats against Bath City and Oxford City, Dorking went on an eight-game unbeaten run towards the end of 2019 before the new year seemed tougher. They only managed to pick up a single point against Billericay Town in January before they followed that with seven points from a possible 18 in February. It didn't get any easier as they lost both games in March before the season was suspended due to the coronavirus pandemic.

Dorking played their last game on 14 March, losing 2-1 at home to Havant & Waterlooville, but despite their poor form they found themselves seventh and in the final play-off spot. Hampton & Richmond sat three points below but had two games in hand. The season was ended but the National League went ahead with play-offs based on points per game. Wealdstone were declared champions and were promoted to the National League (Step 1) while Havant & Waterlooville, Weymouth, Bath City, Slough Town, Dartford and Dorking made the play-offs.

The decision to base the final league standings on a points-per-game basis meant the automatic and promotion spots stayed the same, so no one had missed out, but Hampton & Richmond may have felt hard done by after having games in hand and missing out the play-offs by 0.01 points per game. Had Hampton & Richmond had the opportunities to play their remaining games, Wanderers may have been out of the play-offs, but they didn't sit around to ponder as they prepared for their tie against Bath. The structure of the play-offs meant Slough battled Dartford and Dorking travelled to Bath in the quarter-finals, while second and third, Weymouth and Havant, awaited the winners in the semi-finals.

Dartford eased past Slough with a 3-0 victory on the road while Dorking narrowly beat Bath in the other fixture. Six days later, Dorking lined up against Weymouth and Havant hosted Dartford for a place in the final where the sides would battle for a spot in the tier just below the Football League, the dreamland for any non-league side. Dartford picked up another away win as they beat Havant 2-1, but for Wanderers, it was the end of the road. Weymouth had taken an early 2-0 lead as Josh McQuoid scored from the spot in the third minute before Jaidon Anthony doubled their advantage in eight minutes later. It looked like Weymouth were on course for a comfortable win before goals from James McShane and Elliott Buchanan in the 79th and 85th minutes respectively had brought Wanderers level. The minutes ticked down, but it wasn't to be for White's side as Weymouth pinched a winner in the 95th minute to send them through to the final.

It was tough to take. Although Dorking hadn't expected to be in the play-offs at the start of the season, they knew they were only two games away from reaching yet another new height, but Weymouth had ended their hopes. Still, White was pleased with their first season and was looking towards 2020/21.

'I think it was a fantastic first season because usually, we finish lower down. It was brilliant to finish where we did. It was a bit strange as, off the pitch, we had to pay for COVID testing to ensure we could go ahead with the last few games of the season, which had also put a financial strain and pressure on the club. We managed to pull through in that sense and went into the play-offs. We beat Bath in our first game but lost to Weymouth, so essentially, we finished in the final four of the division. It was tough as we lost to a last-minute goal. It had been a fluke so the manner in which we lost was disappointing, but we were still happy with what we had done that season.'

Ahead of the new season, White set his target out early, knowing exactly where he wanted to finish. There was still some uncertainty before 2020/21, with the pandemic delaying the start, but if the season was definitely going to go ahead White knew he would have to work hard for Dorking to achieve their target.

He said, 'The minimum for us is to reach the play-offs again. I would love to have a title race with whoever is up there towards the end of the season. We had also wanted to have a good FA Cup run, but that came to an end very soon.'

What White had achieved as both manager and chairman was nothing short of spectacular. When he first created Dorking Wanderers, he had done so to enjoy football with mates after he got bored of Premier League football. Twenty-two seasons later, he had achieved something that many clubs only dreamed of in reaching National League South, but he was hoping to better that with a place at the top level of non-league football. His story was inspiring and, while he thought others could replicate his journey, he knew it wouldn't be easy.

'The short answer is yes; anyone can achieve something like this, but the dedication needs to be phenomenal. It's both a financial and physical commitment, and it's doable, but you need a lot of people for support to get through. I've been extremely fortunate that my passion has rubbed off on others and that we've been able to take the club forward as a collective. We've had a lot of people over the years who have helped us immensely and, although they aren't all still involved, they made it all possible.'

Before Wanderers were created, the market town in Surrey celebrated another side, Dorking FC, who were founded in 1880. In their 140 years they had won the Surrey Junior Cup while finishing runners-up twice in the Surrey Senior Cup. They had also reached the first round proper of the FA Cup, losing 3-2 to Plymouth Argyle at Westhumble Playing Fields in 1992/93, but their time was brought to an end when they were dissolved in 2017.

White remains proud of what Wanderers have achieved: 'It's brought our town together. We are a typical modern market town with not much going on. Not many come shopping in the town unless you're getting a haircut, or an Indian takeaway, and it has not had a successful football team for a while. It had certainly brought the community together and we have had a lot of positive comments about that. When I drive to a game now, I can see the families and children in the shirts as they walk to the game, which is a far cry from running a park side when we had to put the nets up ourselves, so they [the fans] play a huge part.'

13

Building for the Future

JUST 19 years of age, Joe Perrett had become an assistant manager in the women's game, joining his dad in managing Harlow Town Ladies. The opportunity had given him the chance to explore the possibility of becoming a coach or manager in his own right, something he wanted to achieve from an early age.

'I always knew that managing and coaching is the avenue I'd like to take in more than playing due to demands on and off the field. I played best when it was fun and with friends, so it was quite apparent to me that I'd like to follow in my dad's footsteps.'

The father-son relationship they shared benefited both parties.

'We share the same philosophy,' Perrett explained. 'We demand the exact same from our players, so we can bounce ideas off each other. We have such a close relationship that we can tell each other when we've gone wrong like if I make a bad decision. If I tell my dad to do something with the tactics and it doesn't go well for the team, he'll tell me, and I'll correct it and look at all the ways I went wrong. A lot of young coaches don't like to take criticism, but where it is my dad, I feel like it's fair criticism, so I can take it on the chin and improve.'

Spending his Sundays working with Harlow Town Ladies was one way Perrett developed his coaching skills, but he also did so in men's football, working with Bishop's Stortford Swifts Reserves. They played in the Essex Olympian League Division Five, below Step 7 and outside of the National League System. It was different from managing women's football, but Perrett wanted to boost his chances of managing at any level of the pyramid.

He said, 'I spent some time at Swifts' reserves, but I learnt how technically different the men's game is to the women's. I've grown up learning about the women's game, so to take the same philosophy is quite challenging and you need to switch your mentality. A lot of the men's players were older than me, so to even get my point across was difficult, but at the same time it was a great learning curve for a young coach like me.'

Before Perrett wanted to coach, he had ambitions to play himself. From the age of 16 he played for Boreham Wood in their academy before also appearing for Sawbridgeworth Town in the Essex Senior League (Step 5). After playing in a professional setup he fell out of love with the game, but the switch to non-league football certainly brought that passion back. It also gave him a chance to explore different pathways to working in football. After a year at National

League Boreham Wood, he didn't have a long spell with the Robins either, finding himself on the bench four times during the 2019/20 season but getting the chance to make substitute appearances. The proudest for him was playing against Hashtag United.

'I enjoyed it [playing for the Boreham Wood academy]. It was like a dream you'd have as a kid to play every day, but there's different aspects of academy football that can drain you and show you the real side of football. That's what can cause you to fall out of love with the game and not want to progress any further. That's really when I started to explore coaching.

'Personally, I don't have any ambitions to play at the moment. Coaching and management is the front-runner for me and that is what I would like to do in football. I wouldn't completely rule out playing, as there is always a pathway back into the game but, right now, sticking with my Dad, coaching in the women's game and getting my badges is the priority.

'The game at lower levels is about passion. The players aren't full-time footballers, so the passion is real. The further you go down the pyramid, it becomes more of a lifeline to people who sometimes struggle. They support their club through everything and continue to support them even if they don't win titles or aren't signing the best players in the league. That's what you call real football.'

At his young age, Perrett had already been trusted to take the reins at Harlow Town Ladies, but under unfortunate circumstances. His Dad had been taken ill, so he stepped up and took charge of their game against Luton. Harlow had been flying in the league but faced a tough test against Luton Town Ladies, who were battling the Hawks for the title.

'It was tough mentally,' he said, thinking back to the game. 'I knew what I was doing with my dad's job while he was in hospital, but it didn't come down to how I was feeling. You had to think about what was going through the players head, who were without their manager and had a young coach taking over. It's hard to think how my dad was feeling in the hospital, wondering about the result and wondering if we had remained unbeaten. It was about the collective unit at Harlow Ladies, and it was tough for everyone. They all showed our true colours [in a good way] and were very supportive.'

The game at the end of September 2019 was won by Harlow and, although it didn't seem important in the title race at the time, as the season was coming to an end the Hawks had opened up a six-point lead at the top. Olivia Steele and Amy Nash scored the goals in a 2-1 victory, which went down as one of Perrett's proudest moments.

'I have two great moments [as a coach]. Beating Luton last season where I took over as manager for a couple of games. That game in particular as we were going neck and neck with them for top spot and were undefeated. The range of emotions I felt throughout that game and to win before driving up and telling him is a feeling that will stick with me forever. That falls above being the youngest ever FA grassroots senior coach of the year nominee.'

Like any sport, it can be hard for young people to break in. Perrett was plotting a path to show what people could achieve. Working alongside his dad was one thing, but it certainly wasn't easy. He had been given a step up but still had to work towards his goal of becoming a coach or manager in his own right.

'I feel like it is becoming more common for more opportunities as a young coach, especially in the women's game. There is more room for improvement as players want to listen and learn and they respect your decision whilst you learn as a coach. In men's football, as a young coach, you might be looked down upon at the start, but you gain ideas and as you gain that experience before stepping into the men's game, I feel like there might be more opportunities coming as a young coach.

'My ambitions right now are to carry on with my dad, to win the [Eastern Region Women's] League, taking the women into the National League, and get my badges done. Once I'm a little older, I want to step forth by either taking over the reins once my dad is done, or branch out, take my own football side, whether that be a reserve side for my dad or a women's team in a lower division. There are plenty of paths to take in football and I'm really excited for the future.'

* * *

When it comes to youth development, different clubs opt for different systems. While professional clubs often choose to go down the route of an academy, many other clubs further down the pyramid opt for reserve teams. Harlow Town were one of those in the latter category.

Although Harlow were playing in the Isthmian League South Central Division (Step 4), their second string played in the reserve league associated with the Essex Senior League (Step 5). The division wasn't part of the National League System, standing alone, so it didn't allow for promotion or relegation to different leagues. This was something that the players needed to understand from early on, as they didn't have the chance to progress up the pyramid, but they did get the chance to develop their game and have the potential to get a first team call-up. For the reserves manager, he didn't think it should affect the mentality of any of the players.

Connolly said, 'Naturally, they should want to win the league, and if we did, they may get noticed [by the first team]. We also have a few cup competitions, but ultimately, the younger players should always try to reach their full potential as we would always relay feedback to the first team. The first-team manager would often come to our games too and the lads are well aware of this. That gives them the platform to always try and get noticed and their chance to make it into the first team.'

The reserves had been entered into the Essex Senior League's reserve division for the 2018/19 season. They had a mixed campaign and finished ninth in a division with 12 clubs, a steady start to life in the league. They were going up against sides who had already established their place in the division: Waltham Abbey Reserves, Grays Athletic

Reserves, Sawbridgeworth Town Reserves and Redbridge Reserves all had a good understanding of the division.

Ahead of the 2019/20 season, Adam Connolly made a step-up from playing in the side to managing the team.

He said, 'This season [2019/20] was my first year in charge of the reserves and my first season in management. I was helping out the team towards the end of the last season before being offered the role towards the end of pre-season when the previous manager stepped down. It's a great club with a good reputation and it feels great to be part of it.

'I played for the reserves for a few games. I knew the manager at the time, Darren Charlton, who was also my manager as a youth player at Barnet. Naturally, it helped me step into the role as manager because it gave me a good understanding of the standard throughout the league. I felt I had a good understanding of the qualities I was looking for in a player in order to compete in the league.'

With promotion and relegation out of the question, Connolly put the development of youth at the forefront of his coaching, preparing players for the potential of a senior call-up. They had silverware they could challenge for, the Reserve Shield and the Peter Butcher Memorial Trophy, on top of challenging for a league title. The Peter Butcher Memorial Trophy was also a cup competition for senior sides in the Essex Senior League, giving the reserves a chance to compete against senior teams. Harlow got a tie against Walthamstow in 2019/20 after Stow had beaten Redbridge Reserves. Reserve sides were entered into the competition automatically, but for the Essex Senior League sides, they were only involved if they lost in the first round of the Gordon Brasted Memorial Trophy. Although winning trophies would always be on his mind, Connolly felt that player development was key to the success of the team.

'It's brilliant [to play senior sides]. We had a tough away fixture last season against Walthamstow. We featured with a young side and were holding them to a draw in the first 40 minutes, but we went on to lose the game 6-1. Regardless of the result, the experience for the team to test themselves against more experienced sides is priceless.

'It's about working with players who are hungry to progress. Every reserve player should have aspirations to play for the first team. It's a great feeling to see one of your players making their debut. We have had a few of our boys doing exactly that and hopefully next season, that will continue. Reserve football should not be the end, it should be a stepping stone.'

When the players did get called up to the first team, even if it was just to train, seeing those lads with the first team would always be a proud moment for Connolly.

'It's a great feeling, almost a proud moment,' he explained. 'It's great to see a clear pathway for the lads. Far too often, reserve and first teams are treated like separate teams. At Harlow, players come here as they know there is great communication between our team and the first team. If you maintain performances, you will get your chance.'

Having a good relationship with the first team meant players were able to feature for the reserves as a means to build fitness, recover from injury or simply to get minutes on the pitch. Providing these opportunities meant the relationship between the sides would strengthen.

Connolly said, 'I've been fortunate enough that in my short spell at the club, I've built a great relationship with the first team. We've seen some players move into the first team, which is what we all want to see, but on the flip side, we've also had several first-team players feature at times to gain much needed minutes.'

Having senior players in the squad was vitally important to the development of young players as they would learn from those who were more experienced. Those players were also leaders and role models.

Connolly added, 'In any side, senior players will always play an important role. They tend to set a good example to our youngsters both on and off the pitch, but it also brings an important balance to the side.'

You only have to look lower down the non-league pyramid to see the possibility of an independent reserve side. The Essex and Suffolk Border League is a good example of reserve teams competing for promotion to rise up the football pyramid. In Division One for 2021/22 are FC Clacton Reserves, Coggeshall United Reserves and Alresford Colne Rangers Reserves. Should Alresford's reserves win promotion then they could find themselves up against the club's first team. Connolly, however, is not looking at having his team rise up – only his players.

'I think the goal and mindset I have while managing a reserve side is completely different. Of course, we want to make every game as competitive as can be, that's what football is about. Having said that, for me, it's about improving the players and preparing them for first-team football. Seeing six of our players playing for Harlow Town in the Isthmian League is what I would call winning.'

Connolly is more than a coach at Harlow Town. As a local man to the club, he is also a supporter and there is no doubt in his heart that he wants the club to do well, on and off the pitch. It was even better for him that he could contribute to the success of the first team, no matter how small his part would be.

'Harlow Town is a great football club. It's also my local club, so I would love nothing more than to see them gain promotion. If I can play a small part of that by having some of my players play their part, it would be even better. I want to bring in more players for pre-season and build a young talented squad.'

He is in the infancy of his managerial career, but has already set out his dreams and what he wants to achieve within the game.

'The last two years have been great. I've learnt a lot in the hot seat and have been fortunate enough to have had some good advice from others, and in particular, Danny Chapman, the current Harlow Town manager. The whole club is fantastic and the whole setup has been very supportive of me since I became manager. I'm still learning and every week, I learn something new about the game, but also about my players.

'Naturally, I hope to step up to first-team level at some point and rise up to the next challenge. As it stands, I'm really enjoying my time at the club and, for now, I am focused on what I need to do in relation to the production of more first-team players, but who knows? One day there may be an opportunity that presents itself that would be too good to turn down.'